MEL

THINKIN(                    ₋ΜΕNT

IN ₋₋HOOLS

# *MEDIATION* AND THINKING DEVELOPMENT IN SCHOOLS

## Theories and Practices for Education

**HEIDI FLAVIAN**
*Achva Academic College, Israel*

United Kingdom – North America – Japan – India
Malaysia – China

Emerald Publishing Limited
Howard House, Wagon Lane, Bingley BD16 1WA, UK

First edition 2019

Published under an exclusive licence

**Reprints and permissions service**
Contact: permissions@emeraldinsight.com

**British Library Cataloguing in Publication Data**
A catalogue record for this book is available from the British
Library

ISBN: 978-1-78756-023-9 (Paperback)
ISBN: 978-1-78756-020-8 (E-ISBN)
ISBN: 978-1-78756-022-2 (Epub)

Printed and bound by CPI Group (UK) Ltd, Croydon, CR0 4YY

ISOQAR certified
Management System,
awarded to Emerald
for adherence to
Environmental
standard
ISO 14001:2004.

ISOQAR
REGISTERED
Certificate Number 1985
ISO 14001

INVESTOR IN PEOPLE

# CONTENTS

# LIST OF GRAPHIC MODELS

# ACKNOWLEDGEMENTS

I would like especially to thank my husband and children, who encouraged me throughout the process of writing this book. In addition, I would like to thank all the researchers and theoreticians who shared their ideas and knowledge with the world and contributed to my understanding of the core meaning of *mediation* and thinking development.

# PREFACE

My understanding that everyone is capable of developing independent thinking skills once they have been guided on how to do so was developed many years before I officially became a teacher, an educator and a mediator. Throughout the three years of high school, once a week, I volunteered as a caregiver of a child who was diagnosed with autism. Although professionals decided that he would not be able to communicate in any way, his parents refused to accept this diagnosis and decided to invite a variety of caregivers who would stimulate him to communicate in different ways. Step by step, it worked and communication slowly developed. Back then I thought it was a miracle, later in life I understood it was *mediation*. Another revelation I experienced was after a few years, as a teacher, during a workshop with Prof. Reuven Feuerstein, who clarified for me the role of the mediator throughout mediatees' thinking development and opened the door for me to the world of *mediation*.

*Mediation* theories were developed for many years to emphasise society's responsibility towards the success of learning among all children, even though the term *mediation* was usually not used. Out of the several twentieth-century learning theories, I have chosen five main theoreticians who approached learning from different perspectives, at different times and in different cultures. The five theories I will focus on in this book are those developed by Dewey, Piaget, Vygotsky,

Feuerstein and Gardner. All five theories include environment, schools and parents in the process of children's learning and thinking development, and they all share the view that children's thinking can be modified. In addition, key results from research in the field of neuropedagogy will be presented to strengthen these theoretical attitudes, since we know today that the brain actually changes as a result of social interactions and interventions. Each perspective discussed here represents a different understanding of society's role in education. Moreover, although these theoreticians did not know each other, their different views of society's role as responsible for all children's development, is the link that may provide educators with a wider and more professional basis for better *mediation*.

While each theoretician believes that his/her theory will be the one to solve most of the dilemmas of education, this book intends to offer practical integration of several existing *mediation* theories. It offers a unique model that integrates different approaches from different periods that can be used effectively by mediators and educators today. Nevertheless, I invite each of the readers to look for other theories and possibilities that also encourage integrating *mediation* for thinking development.

This book offers an opportunity to better understand the role of *mediation* in an era of dynamic social and cultural changes that influence education, in order to better prepare the next generation to become part of society. Hundreds of years ago, ever since leaders of society began to understand the concept of education, the common goal of all was to better educate people in order to make them a productive part of their society in the future. As a result of this broad goal, various approaches to education were developed in order to help individuals become better learners. In other words, theoreticians and researchers studied the human mind and thinking processes in order to develop better and more efficient learning models.

*Mediation*, as mentioned, is a process that promotes learning as a result of learner interactions with the environment. Without reducing the importance of classic learning models, nowadays other goals are at the forefront of the education processes: teachers do not need to keep focussing only on teaching specific disciplines; they also need to focus on knowledge that will be useful in students' future. In addition, students are judged on their achievements in school rather than on their understanding and their thinking development and parents try to help their children excel at school rather than excel as members of society. Although the goals of learning knowledge and reaching new achievements are important, teachers and educators should understand how to mediate knowledge acquisition rather than be the source of knowledge.

*Mediation* processes as mandatory components in education allow all participants to develop better thinking processes. The ideas about *mediation* are wide and cover all areas of life. Therefore, being a great teacher or educator are only two facets of the *mediation* approach. This book will allow all readers to better understand the concept of *mediation*, following with ideas to practice it, and thereby become true mediators.

# *MEDIATION* AND THINKING DEVELOPMENT IN SCHOOLS: THEORIES AND PRACTICES FOR EDUCATION

## INTRODUCTION

The concept of '*mediation*' was originally developed as one of the tools psychologists used in order to allow better communication and processes between them and their patients. But over time, understanding the variety ways *mediation* may be conducted led to possibilities beyond the original notion of the concept. Understanding the role and responsibility of society for individuals' development led a variety of professionals to study the ways *mediation* may be used within different domains. These professionals contributed much knowledge to allow others to improve their communication skills. Nevertheless, *mediation* is a process that needs to be planned and not all human interactions can be defined as *mediation* processes. 'Thinking development' is another concept most people use without understanding its core notion. Whereas the majority of people agree that it is society's responsibility to educate everyone, this consensus is less widespread when it comes to the question of society's responsibility to make sure all people can think well. This is despite the evidence that neuroscientists have shown that the human brain can be modified with the proper stimulation.

From the general perception and understanding of *mediation* along with the possibilities of influencing thinking development, the goal of this book is to share practical ways human can mediate for better thinking development through daily activities both in and out of school.

Throughout this book, the processes of understanding and using *mediation* are presented from the perspectives of psychologists and educators who wished to enhance thinking skills among learners. Although many scholars have dealt with this topic over the years, I have chosen to focus on the five theoreticians that I consider to have paved the way to where we are today.

In the late nineteenth century, Dewey claimed that society's goals should focus on integrating and educating all people within the community and therefore society should treat each individual according to the most efficient way that individual can learn. During the first half of the twentieth century, Piaget developed the *mediation* approach, according to which *mediation* is the core social activity that promotes learning and cognitive activities, although he restricted the effect *mediation* might have on cognitive development to the natural abilities one was born with, cultural differences and age.

Following this theory, both Vygotsky and Feuerstein also developed their theories and addressed *mediation*. Vygotsky focussed on the variety of the types of instruction mediators may provide and on the learning process according to the Zone of Proximal Development of learning along with understanding an individual's culture. Feuerstein, later developed his theory of the Mediated Learning Experience, which also offers practical ways mediators may follow an individual's thinking processes in order to improve them. Feuerstein analysed *mediation* according to 12 parameters, while also categorising thinking processes into 27 cognitive functions, to allow the mediator to better prepare, proceed and follow the success of an individual's cognitive development.

The fifth theoretician presented in this book is Gardner, who developed his theory of multiple intelligences in the 1980s. Gardner's basic argument was that each person thinks using multiple intelligences. Initially Gardner defined seven different intelligences that everyone has, claiming that it was up to the mediators to provide proper processes through which to develop each one. Over the past decade, the field of neuroscience has been greatly expanded by numerous studies that focus on the intentionality between human activity and brain development. Those studies have contributed to the development of the field of neuropedagogy, which integrates knowledge of neuroscience with practical teaching strategies and *mediation*. The neuropedagogical approach is also integrated in this book in order to allow educators to develop learning activities that are also based on updated neuroscience studies. The above approaches will be described in greater detail further on in the book, along with the integration of new practical approaches to pedagogy and teaching.

Even though the theories may seem to differ greatly from one another, there are some common parameters, the most important of which is the essence of the mediators' role. Moreover, according to these theories, mediators are people who wish to better introduce knowledge and processes within the environment to all mediatees. Throughout this book, reference to mediators is from the perspective of educators who are not necessarily officially trained teachers, but are involved in educational processes and wish to promote thinking and learning of any kind.

Wishing to promote all learners' thinking development through conducting better *mediation* processes, this book aims to present the core of each of the abovementioned theories, focussing on the practical possibilities that *mediation* theories offer educators within the environment of school and family. The chapters contain several examples of *mediation*. Although these examples are based on real situations, they present only a small number of mediated situations which should be used as a basis for learning possibilities. Readers may use these examples in order to develop new mediated situations according to their own experiences and their mediatees' cognitive needs.

# 1

# THINKING DEVELOPMENT

Understanding the concept of thinking development relies on integrating a variety of factors that encourage thinking such as the thinking processes the person is conducting, the processes conducted by others in order to inspire that person to think, and the environment that person lives in. Although the fact that humans are thinkers has been always accepted as a fact, theories and studies that allow better understanding of what thinking is and how it develops began no more than 150 years ago. Furthermore, these countless studies led to a variety of approaches each presenting a different definition of thinking. Understanding that there isn't any single truth, educators should recognise and understand different approaches. Only by integrating the core information from each approach with the way educators choose to mediate and teach, can efficient thinking and development appear among their students. As mentioned before, this book presents and examines six approaches that may seem to differ greatly, but all share the core belief that society is responsible for children's thinking development. Five of the approaches in question are those of Dewey, Piaget, Vygotsky, Feuerstein and Gardner. The sixth approach is that of neuropedagogy, which developed from neuroscience studies in order to allow pedagogues to implement updated neuroscience knowledge within educational studies and processes.

## 1.1. JOHN DEWEY (1859–1952)

John Dewey was born in the USA in 1859 and although he was a highly influential American social and political philosopher, he became best known as the philosopher who developed new educational theories and approaches (Dewey, 1938/2015). One of his main academic contributions was making psychologists aware that their studies should become the foundation of educational practices and the development of new pedagogical approaches; otherwise there was no logic in conducting those studies (Jackson, 1990). From this point of view, Dewey founded laboratory schools adjacent to the university, claiming that the role of researchers should be to look at human nature and apply it to the school system rather than focussing in schools on teaching knowledge without understanding human thinking processes.

Investigating learning processes from a psychological standpoint, looking at the changes in society from philosophical perspectives, and the desire to develop better schools that better prepare learners for independent adult life were the main factors that led to the development of the experimental education approach and the establishment of the experimental schools. Dewey's point of view that education is a dynamic progress that should be examined and reformed according to the results of practicing education also changed the role of teachers. Teachers, who were used only to delivering information, had to ask themselves what activities would motivate their students to investigate their environment in a manner that would allow them to learn the same information on their own (Dewey, 1938/2015). When Dewey was asked by educators on what philosophy he based his educational approach, his answer was: 'The scientific method by means of which man studies the world, acquires cumulatively knowledge of meaning and values' (Dewey, 1938/2015, p. 10). But, although it may look simple, Dewey also claimed that a planned education reform should be conducted in order to allow such educational experiences and development.

In practice, Dewey challenged schools to motivate learners to think, to investigate, and to learn on their own from the environment in order to create better thinkers and independent learners in the future. He believed that new concepts and ideas should be integrated along with practicing them and creating a dynamic process of learning. The efficacy of those new concepts is examined by their link to what was in the past and how they provided opportunities to discover new knowledge.

As mentioned, according to Dewey's perspective, teachers should understand that their role was no longer to be expert in a specific domain and teach the relevant knowledge, but rather mediate society's norms and rules of behaviour in order to prepare learners for the future. Based on the understanding that any education system's goal is to allow better social integration in adulthood, teachers cannot base their learning interactions on teaching knowledge that might not be relevant for the learners as they grow up. Dewey believed that teachers had to become experts in understanding human behaviour and human thinking development, and become the ones who create opportunities for learners to investigate and develop.

While pushing society to change the education system, Dewey (1938/2015) contrasted his idea of progressive education with traditional education by emphasising the following six key criteria:

(1) *Teachers as models of society*: Since teachers interact with students through most of their learning time, they should understand that they 'are the agents through which knowledge and skills are communicated and rules of conduct are enforced' (Dewey, 1938/2015, p. 18). Accordingly, teachers should be familiar with social changes around them, and prepare their students to learn what they do not yet know. If teachers teach only what they know, they will tie knowledge to the past without developing the thinking skills necessary to solve the as yet unknown.

(2) *School organisation*: From the perspective of traditional schools as the core of learning knowledge, educators of the progressive approach should realise that school organisation does not in any way resemble any other family or social organisation in the society children grow up in, and therefore understanding or adjusting to the school organisation does not prepare understanding or adaptation to any other organisation children encounter on a daily basis. Therefore, learning should be conducted most of the time outside the schools premises, in the environment where learners live.

(3) *Quality of experience*: Success and quality of learning according to progressive education is evaluated by the influence on success in learning and adjusting in the future. Whereas traditional educators evaluate students according to specific expected standards which focus on repeating what was studied, progressive education challenges evaluation through dealing with new situations. From that perspective, progressive teachers should always ask themselves whether or not the experience they have planned prepares their students for new situations in life. Moreover, the quality

of experience within progressive education is more important than its quantity.

(4) *Children's experiences*: Progressive education is based on the understanding that children need to experience, to investigate, ask, look for answers and not to learn facts and evidence other people have researched for them. Although traditional education includes a variety of classroom experiences, they are strict, well formatted, and controlled by the teachers and the environment with expected specific results according to the discipline in which the experience was conducted.

(5) *Individual progress of learning*: Dewey challenged progressive education teachers to understand that each learner may develop at a different pace. Learning processes develop according to the opportunities the child has to investigate and according to the *mediation* the child receives from the surrounding society. Learning is a process that every child undergoes at a different pace but in the same direction. For any group of learners, educators must plan different opportunities for learning for different children, that is, differential *mediation*. Moreover, when learning does not progress properly, educators must observe and ask themselves what other experiences the learners should undergo and which learning environment will provide the best opportunity for learning. Intervention and direct teaching should be initiated only when all other possibilities fail to provide results.

(6) *The freedom to learn*: Dewey based the model of progressive schools on studies that demonstrated how thinking skills develop as one experiences learning and solving problems in a variety of situations. To this end, learners must have high intrinsic motivation to

learn and confront challenging assignments. Such
motivation can only develop when learners choose the
domain they want to study. Nevertheless, in traditional
schools teachers choose which subjects and topics to
teach, deciding when and how to teach them. Dewey
(1938/2015) summarised this by saying:

> *We are taught the basis of democracy by schools,*
> *by press, the pulpit, the platform, our lawmakers*
> *and our laws, and … our parents and everyone*
> *within the society …. We are taught to choose our*
> *experiences and thoughts in a democratic way …*
> *but schools do not allow real choices – they tell us*
> *what choices are right and wrong. (p. 33)*

Dewey invited everyone to think how to improve education
so all learners and teachers would retain their natural curios-
ity and eagerness to learn, along with developing their thinking skills. Nevertheless, he emphasised that changes should
not eliminate the existing school system but rather retain the
positive factors and develop from there. Moreover, educators
should remember that education is a never-ending process. It
is the type of job that is never completed because it is the basis
for every group of people wishing to become a better society.
In sum, Dewey challenged educators to integrate all individuals
while developing a united culture. He expressed this challenge
through his pedagogical creed by stating:

> *I believe that the individual who is to be educated*
> *is a social-individual and that society is an organic*
> *union of individuals. If we eliminate the social*
> *factor from the child we are left only with an*
> *abstraction; if we eliminate the individual factor*
> *from society, we are left only with an inert and*
> *lifeless mass. (Dewey, 1897, p. 78)*

## 1.2. JEAN PIAGET (1896–1980)

Jean Piaget was born in Switzerland in 1896 and was known as a psychologist who focussed on child development. His cognitive theory of learning developed after a long period of study on biological species, their classification, and how they adapt to different situations in nature (Harris, 1997). Piaget associated the development of species with the adaptation of human intelligence by claiming that the ways in which organisms interact with their environment lead to ever more successful adaptation in the future. He is also known as one of the earliest and most cogent researchers who initiated the controversy surrounding the psychometric and behaviourist approaches to intelligence, claiming that society can influence human intelligence (Feuerstein, Feuerstein, Falik, & Rand, 2006). Moreover, Piaget claimed that one of the reasons for the lack of understanding of the meaning of cognition, thinking and intelligence was the narrow approach researchers had based their theories on.

Piaget developed and defined a learning model based on direct exposure to and interaction with the environment. The model symbolises the process in which direct stimuli reach an organism (learner), and the organism is expected to respond accordingly. This structure of learning is the basis for changes within the learners' cognitive processes, due to the variety of stimuli they interact with and their responses. Nevertheless, the intent of the environment to provide stimuli is not enough, since learners must be amenable to absorb the stimuli and learn from them.

Therefore, the more interaction one has with the environment the better cognitive skills one has to adapt to new situations. While referring specifically to cognitive development, Piaget suggested that learning is a process of adaptation in which leaners seek equilibrium by integrating new information into existing structured knowledge, and create possibilities for new structured information by comparing new and existing information (Willis, 2007).

Although Piaget disagreed with those who claimed intelligence was fixed at birth, and although he encouraged creating opportunities to practice learning and improve cognitive skills, he also claimed that intelligence developed in blocks according to specific stages. Piaget defined three main stages he believed all humans undergo as cognition and intelligence develop. Piaget emphasised that the order of the stages is crucial, and one cannot skip a stage and go back to it later in life. The basic stage of thinking is characterised by preoperational activities based mainly on the evaluation of sensorimotor development and in which visual symbols are used. The importance of this stage as presented in learning processes is that the children experience learning by imitating their environment. The cyclical reactions evolving from repetitive interactions with objects, events and people are refined and modified through these activities and therefore the environment is responsible for the broadening of learning schema from birth (Feuerstein et al., 2006). Following the sensorimotor period is the concrete stage in which children learn how to generalise actions, differentiate between past and present, and learn how to operate simple physical objects. The third stage is formal thinking through which one can form hypotheses, solve problems, deal with abstract ideas, and develop logical reasoning (White, 2006). Although the organised logic and processes described through the stages are clear, Piaget claimed that the differences between leaners of the same age may result from different opportunities society allows them to experience. Thus, thinking develops according to a clear path but at a different pace.

The influence of social interactions on one's thinking development is also expressed in Piaget's explanation of human intelligence. Piaget (1947/2001) claimed that the nature of intelligence is based on the integration of biological and logical processes, along with the social interactions one experiences. Nevertheless, not all social interactions are effective enough to influence cognitive development. To conduct an effective interaction, it has to be planned and structured along with proper energetics to implement the process (Piaget, 1966/2000).

Piaget's approach towards thinking development and the role of society in one's development was derived from his studies in biology. Nevertheless, when questioning the process of human thinking development he considered the role of society to be a significant factor. As mentioned, Piaget defined three critical stages in cognitive development based on biological and neurological developments. However, these stages are only the basis and the role of society from birth is to provide proper possibilities to develop from there on. Within his theory, Piaget criticised the overemphasis of psychoanalysis on the aspects of thinking processes, and claimed that the essence of intelligence lies in its active constructions by the individual. As Piaget phrased the interactions between all factors:

> *Society ... changes the very structure of the individual ... it not only compels him to recognize facts ... modify his thoughts ... it imposes on him an infinite series of obligations. It is therefore quite evident that social life affects intelligence. (Piaget, 1947/2001, p. 171)*

## 1.3. LEV VYGOTSKY (1896–1934)

Lev Vygotsky was born in the Russian Empire, and was known as a revolutionary psychologist. The main radical change he made was defining the concept of 'cultural psychology', in which he focussed on human beings as objects that are changed more by cultural processes than by natural ones (Kozulin, 1999).

His theory of thinking development in reference to intelligence and human *mediation* was based on the integration of human culture alongside bio-social development. Within his revolutionary theory of thinking development, Vygotsky emphasised that any planned process of social intervention through one's learning development, promotes both intelligence and cognitive modifiability, and that different people think differently mostly because of differences in the *mediation* they have experienced (Daniels, 2016). Vygotsky is also known in relation to the field of positive psychology, given his claim that everyone can learn with proper social intervention. His approach towards learning and cognitive development requires mediators to focus on the human mind and to look for learners' uniquely mental processes in order to mediate according to the cognitive strengths and needs of the mediatees (Feuerstein et al., 2006). This perspective is also reflected in his suggestion that cognitive assessments should focus also on emergent cognitive functions that can be revealed only in the course of problem solving shared with and assisted by adults, in order to learn about the how children learn from their environment.

The three significant factors in Vygotsky's positive psychology are: the culture people live in, the people participating in that society, and the learners. Regarding culture, Vygotsky claimed that any change in psychological process is related to changes in sociocultural types of *mediation*. Furthermore, he emphasised that the history of each culture also causes changes within the vocabulary, which then affect the psychological functions that relate to reading, writing and mathematical reasoning. These changes of language, which are no doubt cultural, granted the status of cognitive functions, and are fundamental faculties of intelligence, memory, imagination and independent learning (Kozulin, 1999).

While Vygotsky based his claim that culture is the most significant factor influencing one's cognitive development, he specifically addressed society and the individual within it. The integration between these factors involved proposing that the structure of *mediation* is shaped by the human use of signs, symbols and language, all of which are cultural. Following the approach of psychological development, Vygotsky explained the transition from natural forms of behaviour all humans are born with to higher mental functions humans may develop through structured *mediation*. He also explained that undergoing different *mediation* processes, with different people and different degrees of complexity might lead to different cognitive development among learners (Daniels, 2016; Kozulin, 1999). Moreover, Vygotsky strongly claimed that the development of higher mental processes relies mainly on functions of mediated activity.

Vygotsky's main claim was that the extent to which, how and when individuals realise their potential is highly affected by the type of mediated learning they experience. Moreover, he insisted that human potential for cognitive development may move beyond what others have evaluated and may be expressed in situations that are far from the original learning situation. But, to succeed in this cognitive development process, the role of the mediatees – the learners – is significant. They must be active throughout the process and should be aware of the learning and the changes.

Vygotsky described how far one can advance in any learning experience through the model of the 'Zone of Proximal Development' (ZPD). This term describes the difference between what learners can learn spontaneously and independently, what they are able to learn with *mediation*, and how they may use the new knowledge they have learned with *mediation* in other situations (Daniels, 2016; Kozulin, 1999). The main message Vygotsky aimed to disseminate was the fact the society has the opportunity to change and develop people's cognitive skills, and therefore society should do its best to create independent thinkers.

## 1.4. REUVEN FEUERSTEIN (1921–2014)

Reuven Feuerstein was born in Romania, and after accomplishing his psychologist studies in Romania, Geneva and Paris, he continued his research and studies around the world while living in Israel.

From his experience with children from different cultures and his knowledge in psychology and learning, Feuerstein developed the theory of Mediated Learning Experience (MLE) followed by his theory of Structural Cognitive Modifiability (SCM). Both theories were developed from the belief that all humans can change cognitively as a result of the *mediation* they receive from other humans in their environment (Feuerstein, 2001). While other psychologists and educators at that time spoke about a variety of ways children learn from their interactions with the environments, Feuerstein emphasised the differences between direct exposures to stimuli whereas no adult follows the learning processes and learning that occurs through deliberately mediated interactions that mediators plan according to specific needs of the mediatees (Feuerstein, Mintzker, & Feuerstein, 2001). Moreover, Feuerstein suggested that individuals are capable of meaningful structural changes resulting from the development of their cognitive abilities and skills. But, these structural changes can occur only through different types of open systems, by experiencing proper *mediation* from the adults around them (Van Der Aalsvoort, Resing, & Ruijssemaars, 2002). After studying human thinking processes, and in order to allow mediators to plan and conduct efficient *mediation* experiences, Feuerstein also analysed and defined 27 specific cognitive-functions that humans need to use while learning (Feuerstein, Feuerstein, Falik, & Rand, 2002). These cognitive functions are organised according to two main criteria. First, they are categorised according to the three phases of thinking: input, elaboration and output. Then, within each stage of thinking, the cognitive functions are organised from the basic mandatory cognitive function needed to conduct that phase of thinking to the more complex ones. In addition, Feuerstein defined each as a good cognitive function versus a deficient function, in order to clarify the kind of *mediation* that is needed. The original 27 cognitive functions Feuerstein defined are as follows:

### 1.4.1. The Input Phase

The functions of the input phase determine the quality of the data gathered by the learner and therefore influence the quality of the entire thinking process. Feuerstein defined eight cognitive functions that are essential at this thinking phase:

(1) Clear perception versus blurred and sweeping perception.

(2) Systematic exploration versus unplanned, impulsive and unsystematic exploration cognitive behaviour.

(3) Precise and accurate labelling versus lack of, or impaired verbal receptive tools that affect discrimination.

(4) Well-developed orientation in space versus lack of, or impaired spatial orientation and lack of stable systems of reference that impair the establishment of topological and Euclidean organisation of space.

(5) Well-developed orientation in time versus lack of, or impaired temporal concepts.

(6) Conservation of constancies versus lack of, or impaired conservation of constancies of factors such as size, shape, quantity etc.

(7) Need for precision, accuracy and completeness in data gathering versus lack of, or deficient need for precision and accuracy in data gathering.

(8) Capacity to consider more than one source of information versus lack of capacity to consider two or more sources of information at once.

### 1.4.2. The Elaboration Phase

Through the elaboration phase the individual needs to integrate all the information gathered during the input phase and use it properly in order to create relevant knowledge. Feuerstein defined 11 cognitive functions that humans should use while elaborating:

(1) Accurate definition of the problem versus inadequacy in the perception of the existence and definition of an actual problem.

(2) Selection of relevant cues versus inability to differentiate between relevant and irrelevant information.

(3) Spontaneous comparative behaviour versus lack of spontaneous comparative behaviour.

(4) Broad mental field and memory versus narrowness of the mental field.

(5) Integrating a variety of data from different domains and learning situations versus an episodic grasp of reality.

(6)  Using logical evidence to arrive at and defend conclusions versus lack of or impaired need to pursue logical evidence.

(7)  Internalisation of information versus lack of internalisation of information.

(8)  Inferential hypothetical thinking versus lack of or impaired inferential, hypothetical thinking.

(9)  Use of strategies for hypothesis testing versus lack of or impaired strategies for hypothesis testing

(10) Planning behaviour versus lack of or impaired planning behaviour

(11) Use of adequate verbal tools and elaboration of certain cognitive categories versus use of inadequate verbal tools to organise the data.

### 1.4.3. The Output Phase

After adequately gathering data and appropriate elaboration, proper communication of the final results should be conducted as well. Feuerstein defined eight cognitive functions that are responsible for this phase of thinking:

(1)  Using clear and precise language versus using egocentric communicational modalities.

(2)  Projection of virtual relationships versus difficulty in projecting virtual relationships.

(3)  Communicating the answer versus blocking despite knowing the answer.

(4)  Thinking things through before responding versus using trial and error behaviour.

(5) Using adequate verbal tools versus using inadequate verbal tools for communicating adequately elaborated responses.

(6) Precision and accuracy versus lack of precision and accuracy in communicating data and information.

(7) Clear visual transport versus deficiency in visual transport.

(8) Waiting before responding versus impulsivity and acting-out behaviour.

Understanding thinking processes according to the three phases and the 27 cognitive functions provided Feuerstein with a solid basis for further investigation of human thinking development and the influence of society on cognitive changes. Feuerstein stressed this approach by claiming the society may influence and contribute to people's thinking development furthermore than the genetic basis they were born with. From a broad-spectrum, Feuerstein's Mediated Learning Experience, describes the contribution of adults to transferring the principles of one learning situation to another by discussing the process and the principles involved with the mediatees (learners), in order to extract meaning from the specific situation and make the experience intentional (Feuerstein, 2001).

Based on the approach that a society influence one's thinking development, Feuerstein defined human's intelligence as the individual's ability to utilise experience in order to better learn from and adjust to new situations. This approach towards the meaning of intelligence and cognitive development emerged also from criticising the IQ tests, which Feuerstein claimed were based on testing prior knowledge rather than a person's ability to learn. In addition, Feuerstein claimed that the standard IQ test emphasised one's difficulties in learning rather than the positive potential to think (Van Der Aalsvoort et al., 2002). Beyond criticising the standard IQ test, Feuerstein developed dynamic assessment of cognitive modifiability; the Learning Potential Assessment Device (LPAD), which enables understanding of individual learning processes and the way thinking changes as a result of human *mediation* (Kozulin, 1998). Throughout the cognitive assessment, LPAD allows mediators to detect cognitive functions that may not be functioning as they should. Accordingly, they are expected to conduct specific *mediation* and intervention processes and to re-assess the same cognitive functions in new situations. The *mediation* process must be conducting according to the 12 criteria of the MLE theory in order to maintain common language among all MLE mediators (all 12 criteria are presented in part 2.3.1 in this book). This process of assessing, mediating and re-assessing provides the possibilities to follow the efficiency of the mediated interactions for better thinking development. Following the LPAD, Feuerstein also developed an educational programme focussing on developing thinking skills and cognitive functions and that is based on human *mediation*. Feuerstein called this programme Instrumental Enrichment (IE) to emphasise that thinking is a tool every human possesses and that the role of the mediators is to make sure everyone has the opportunity for proper thinking development. After understanding that thinking skills are the basic tools for all types of thinking, through this programme, mediators integrate mediated learning experiences to develop and strength all cognitive functions (Feuerstein, 2002). Both the LPAD and the IE developed as part of the MLE and cannot be conducted without believing in the potential for cognitive changes among all, nevertheless they cannot proceed without conducting proper *mediation*.

For the broad perspective and use of the term *mediation*, and in order to allow educational mediators to reflect on the *mediation* processes they participated in, Feuerstein et al. (2006) distinguished regular teaching from *mediation* by defining 12 significant criteria (these will be explained in Chapter 2). Furthermore, Feuerstein insisted that human *mediation* and intervention have much more influence on cognitive development than any genetic basis one may be born with.

Following the SCM approach, along with understanding the power humans have on others' thinking development, mediators should also believe in people's ability to be modified and changed as a result of their *mediation*. This is the basis for becoming skilled mediators.

This implies that mediators need to plan learning interactions and experiences by integrating their understanding of the role of the cognitive functions along with the criteria of *mediation* in order to contribute to the process of mediatees' cognitive development.

## 1.5. HOWARD EARL GARDNER (1943–)

Howard Gardner was born in the USA, and is known as an American developmental psychologist. Among the many researchers and theoreticians of education and thinking development, Gardner is known as one of the main revolutionaries (Feuerstein et al., 2006). Gardner evolved his theory, claiming that the standard psychometric assessments of intelligence offer educators a very narrow understanding of human thought processes. Gardner also claimed that as long as researchers do not differentiate between natural, innate talent and intelligence, which is assessed through activities that researchers believe properly reflect it, true understanding of thinking development will not occur. According to his understanding that intelligence is represented by several skills, he defined different types of intelligences in relation to different types of thinking skills and contexts, and proposed following the development of intelligence accordingly. The main concept Gardner contributed to psychologists and educators is 'multiple intelligences'. With this concept Gardner emphasised that not only does every human learn and present his knowledge using as variety of intelligences, but also that educators must teach and assess learning in variety of ways. Moreover, Gardner claimed that development of the different types of intelligence is a result of the *mediation* one experiences, and that society influences ones intellectual development further than anyone can predict (Gardner, 2011). While referring to the cultural differences among people that may cause the intellectual differences, Gardner (2000) explained that these differences prove the responsibility of society for developing efficient thinkers and learners. From his perspective, it is only when society understands the importance of investing in schools and therefore taking care of developing thinkers in several ways that new and true learners can develop in that society. He claimed that children are born with all they need in order to be educated and independent thinkers, and it is only up to the society they are mediated in to provide their cognitive needs.

Analysing human thinking processes and cognitive development led Gardner (2011) to define seven types of intelligences that human use while thinking. However, one of his main arguments is that all people are born with basic skills to use all seven, and it is only up to society how each child will learn to use them, and which of them will be the most efficient intelligence used. In addition, although most people are recognised as having only one specific intelligence they use extremely well, the seven intelligences are simultaneously in process all the time and contribute to each other. The seven intelligences are:

(1)  *Logical/mathematical intelligence*: Gardner defined logical- mathematical intelligence as all thinking processes connected with logic, abstractions, reasoning, numbers and critical thinking. This area includes mainly the ability to logically analyse, compare, describe and conclude process on the basic of logic. It is also includes the capacity to understand the underlying principles of some kind of casual system.

(2)  *Linguistic/verbal intelligence*: The link between the development of language and thinking processes has known for many years and researchers have described it in studies over the past two decades. Nevertheless, Gardner referred to linguistic intelligence as a unique area in which people use the language not only to communicate and to learn, but also to create new knowledge. Educators can detect children with high verbal-linguistic intelligence by following their facility for words and languages. They are also typically good at reading, writing, telling stories and memorising words and dates.

(3)  *Musical/rhythmic intelligence*: Musical intelligence includes the sensitivity to sounds, rhythms, tones and music. People with high musical intelligence normally have good or even absolute pitch. People, who are identified with high musical intelligence are likely to excel at singing, playing musical instruments, or composing music.

(4)  *Spatial/visual intelligence*: The cognitive ability to visualise and act according to surrounding information is a basic ability for learning. On the basis of this intelligence babies learn how to plan their movements around objects, and later learn to read, but it is mostly

significant for spatial judgment and the ability to visualise from the abstract perception when the objects are not concrete such as using geographic maps to plan routes and to get from one place to another.

(5) *Bodily/kinesthetic intelligence*: Understanding that controlling body movements requires a high level of cognitive skill led Gardner to define bodily–kinesthetic skill as one of the intelligences. The core meaning is that beyond the capacity to handle objects skilfully, bodily–kinesthetic intelligence also includes a sense of timing to create proper movement and respond to others' movements. Accordingly, people who have high bodily–kinesthetic intelligence can be highly successful in a variety of physical activities such as sports, dance and acting.

(6) *Interpersonal intelligence*: Living in a society and developing through proper socialisation processes requires specific cognitive skills, which Gardner characterised as interpersonal intelligence. The elements of this intelligence feature the sensitivity a person has towards other people with whom he or she interacts. This cognitive process refers to the effective communication people conduct as a result of understanding others' moods, feelings, temperaments and motivations. People with high interpersonal intelligence are recognised by their ability to cooperate in order to work as a part of a group, present effective empathy and be motivated to improve through the social activities around them.

(7) *Intrapersonal intelligence*: Having all the necessary cognitive skills is only the basis to be able to operate them efficiently. The unique intrapersonal intelligence

Garden defined refers to the cognitive skills that develop deep understanding of the self. This unique understanding develops from an understanding of the cognitive strengths or weaknesses one may have, and how to use them effectively to learn better. Moreover, this intelligence allows one better activation of all the other six mentioned intelligences.

Since Gardner first published the multiple intelligences theory, other researchers have offered to add additional types of intelligences to the original seven. Although Gardner (2011) did not reject their idea immediately, he argued that any additional intelligence offered must include the following three criteria the original seven: (a) must appear among all people; (b) must function simultaneously with all the basic seven intelligences; (c) with proper *mediation*, most people will be able to present efficient use of it. Following Gardner's criteria, none of the offers were accepted as separate new types of intelligences, but as sub-intelligences that some people may present extremely unique use of.

## 1.6. THE NEUROPEDAGOGY APPROACH

The field of neuroscience has developed from scientists' drive to better understand how the brain works. After many years of conducting numerous studies, neuroscientists can better analyse all parts of the human brain and explain the role of each part, the coordination between all the parts and their impact on brain functions. These understandings were the basis for the development of two other fields; neuropsychology and educational-neuroscience. While the goal of neuroscientists is to better understand brain functions, the neuropsychologists' vision is to develop a cognitive neuroscience that is educationally relevant along with integrating all the necessary knowledge related to brain mechanisms that may promote better learning (Berninger & Abbott, 1992). Over the years, the fundamental goal of educational neuroscientists has become focussed on establishing an added value that studying the brain brings to educational questions. Moreover, educational neuroscientists like to challenge their studies in order to better understand the impact of real-world learning on brain activities and how this information can be better applied to academic skill acquisition (Rosenberg-Lee, 2018).

The field of neuroscience developed towards the end of the nineteenth century, and we learn today that the concept of Executive Functions (EF) was in used already in the 1840s while researchers were examining the frontal lobes and the prefrontal cortex (Barkley, 2012). Most of the brain-studies that focussed of the ways it functions initiated from situations whereas people demonstrated disability to function as others. From the same point of view, while trying to understand the reasons for learning disabilities, neuroscientists realised that within the complexity of the brain specific functions are responsible for learning processes. At the same time researchers also realised that despite the brain's fragility, it also is uniquely resilient in the presence of genetic or environmental influences, and the ability to change and overcome dysfunctions when specific intervention is conducted (Moyes, 2014). From these studies, researchers in the field of neuroscience, psychology and education integrated the EF into their explanations in regard to how our brain conducts learning and thinking. The EF concept describes specific processes performed by the brain while thinking, and the questions asked since then have been about how the EF work, whether they can be influenced by a variety of factors, and how can scientists follow their normal and abnormal development. The EF became familiar concepts and were used as common criteria for numerous researchers who conducted their studies from different perspectives and with different goals. In recent decades, both neuroscientists and educational neuroscientists have focussed their studies on the neurological processes that occur in the brain during learning. With the massive development of technology and neuroimaging possibilities, researchers conduct new studies that allow better understanding of general brain functions, along with specific examinations of cognitive functions such as memory processes, general learning, the links between emotions and learning, and between motor development and learning (Zull, 2011). Those studies and the desire to use our brains better has led to closer cooperation between neuroscientists and educational-neuroscientists, who realised that understanding how the brain works is the basis for a new field of research. From this point, educators, pedagogues and researchers from other fields came together and neuropedagogy began to develop.

The cooperation among the various researchers from different domains focussing on one common goal—to better understand how the brain develops and functions—required proper use of the main concepts of each domain and the creation of new concepts where needed. Nevertheless, the unique core goal of neuropedagogy, from the point of view of how to better teach our learners to use their brain, is to keep examining how the brain operates, what cognitive and executive functions take part in different learning situations, and how to teach according to this knowledge.

Beyond the deep understanding of the variety of ways the brain functions while learning, one of the major contributions of the neuroscience and the neuropedagogy is the understanding of the influence of the environment on one's thinking processes, which are the brain's dynamic changes. Weinbaum and Veitas (2017) describe their journey of understanding the meaning of intelligence and the ways our brain develops by beginning with the basic philosophy of learning as individuals in a dynamic environment. They explored Aristotle's theory, which claimed that individuals cannot develop individuation and become thinkers without interacting with the people around them (Weinbaum & Veitas, 2017). Then, by studying who the intelligent people are and what may be the unique way their brains work, they discovered the variety of approaches towards the meaning of intelligence and how society changes the definitions according to their goals. The main conclusion of their research is the understanding that not only is the brain the most advanced intelligent machine we know, but it is also the most interactive, changing and developing from the endless interaction with the environment and surrounding people. The brain and thinking are developed as result of the dynamic feedback people receive from their surroundings, along with their need to cope with unfamiliar situations. Therefore, in order to contribute to thinking development it is necessary to learn about brain functions, along with on-going interactions with the learners and the provision of a variety of opportunities for thinking challenges, new situations, questions and dilemmas with uncertain answers.

As presented throughout this chapter, each theoretician developed a different learning theory based on studies and experiences. What is common to all these theoreticians and theories is the emphasis on the power society has to modify and develop each individual's thinking processes, and consequently the responsibility society has to promote such development. Another common criterion found in all the above approaches is that efficient learning is expressed when learners apply their thinking in domains other than those in which they initially gained their knowledge. The following model presents the essence of each learning approach, focussing on the link between human *mediation* and thinking development (Model 1).

**Model 1:   The Role of Human *Mediation* in
Learning Theories.**

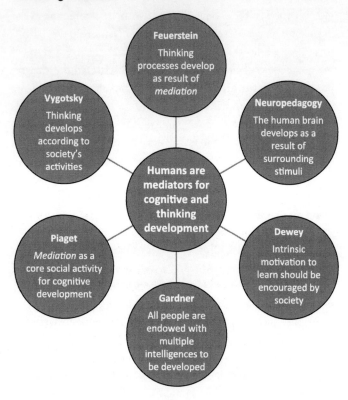

# 2

## *MEDIATION*: A UNIQUE EDUCATIONAL PROCESS

Looking for the broad meaning of *mediation* leads towards a general process according to which people communicate in order to transfer ideas, thoughts, knowledge, or information. Usually, this involves one person who is responsible for whatever he or she would like to transfer, and the process which may be performed in any form of communication (writing, speaking, drawing, dancing, etc.). Assessing whether or not the information was received correctly is not mandatory, and it is up to the person to decide whether to do so. Moreover, in some cases the goal of the *mediation* will be only to express abstract ideas, as in dance, art, or theatre, and therefore the people who receive the *mediation* may have subjective point of view and understanding. In contrast, when mediating in educational contexts, reciprocal communication is mandatory and the role of mediator is thus much more than delivering messages.

## 2.1. *MEDIATION*, TEACHING AND LEARNING

The first chapter presented six different approaches to allow a broader yet deeper understanding of thinking development that occurs as a result of societal influences. In the light of these theories, there is a consensus among educators and researchers regarding the role of society as a significant factor for children's cognitive development. The power of society to change and to improve cognitive development is no longer a topic of debate (Flavian, 2017), although only professional educators conduct it, rather than everyone. However, from this educational perspective there is now a greater challenge for educators: the challenge of conducting quality *mediation* processes as an integral part of their educational routine.

Integrating *mediation* on a daily basis throughout all school activities requires more than merely learning about the approach of *mediation*. One of the challenges educators may have while integrating *mediation* into their daily work is first to distinguish between teaching-learning and *mediation*. For the purpose of this book, the differentiation between these concepts will follow wide-ranging explanations accepted by the majority of educators.

The concepts of teaching and learning are used in order to describe processes through which specific knowledge is studied for the purpose of becoming knowledgeable in a certain domain of information. Whereas general learning can be through both direct and indirect processes, while referring to learning in schools most of the processes conducted indirect according to the planned intervention of the teachers. These learning processes are conducted both when general academic skills are taught such as reading or writing, and when the learners focus on becoming excellent in using those skills. Keeping in mind that educators can also plan the opportunities to promote their learners' thinking development, there should be also a focus on thinking skills throughout curricula specifically while teaching basic academic skills such as reading and writing, but also throughout all subjects matters (Haywood, 2004). Another teaching-learning situation usually occurs when concrete disciplines are studied, such as geography or history. These two examples present situations in which the teacher enriches learners' knowledge and academic skills, and the learner becomes more knowledgeable in those domains. Nevertheless, the teaching-learning methods do not expand beyond the curriculum topic.

In contrast, when educators use the term *mediation*, they are referring to a different viewpoint of learning. *Mediation* in general, and specifically in this book, refers to the processes in which mediators and mediatees cooperate in order for the mediatees to become independent thinkers and learners by using their new knowledge beyond the situation in which it was first acquired. Through *mediation*, every topic or academic skill is studied at first from the perspective of the mediatees, along with the possible uses they may make of it after the learning situation is over. The learners' perspectives may differ as a result of their different background, culture, cognitive skills, or any other factor that may influence their learning. Nevertheless, the mediators' goal is to mediate in a way that thinking develops much further than the where the mediatees began.

The processes of teaching-learning and *mediation* yield different results, given their different goals and different perspectives in regard to the role of education. However, it should be noted that any *mediation* involves a stage of teaching and learning, while not every teaching-learning situation integrates *mediation*.

*Mediation* has only become a key concept in education work in recent decades, even though the idea of *mediation* was in use many years earlier. Hundreds of years ago, before the field of teaching became a profession one needed to be trained for, the role of the teacher as a social leader was already acknowledged.

The first known philosopher who spoke about the role of teachers and the process of teaching was Socrates who claimed that his role was to make sure his students had the tools to learn by themselves (Sellars, 2014). Moreover, his claim was that he did not possess any knowledge whatsoever and therefore could not teach any knowledge. Socrates' main argument was that knowledge exists everywhere and it is up to the teachers to make sure learners investigate their surroundings and ask questions on their own. Without using the term, Socrates actually made people conscious of the idea of *mediation* and their role as mediators.

## 2.2. *MEDIATION* AS A KEY FOR THINKING DEVELOPMENT

Nowadays, educators use *mediation* as a general concept to describe the process in which people present their ideas, thoughts, content, or anything else they would like to share with others. Although the core meaning of *mediation* and the variety of ways in which educators use this term may slightly differ among professionals, the main goal for all is common; to develop better thinking and learning among learners. Beyond the basic process of *mediation*, it is the educators' responsibility to maintain intrinsic motivation for learning among all learners. Moreover, when learners do not possess the drive to search for new knowledge, educators should look for the reason for the learners' resistance and resolve it in order to restore their natural desire to learn (Kozulin & Rand, 2000).

The understanding that according to the theories of cognitive development educators can mediate for better thinking and cognition among their students led many researchers to conduct studies tracing the development of thinking skills and processes among learners and in order to develop better curricula.

Shayer and Adhami (2010) conducted their study while focussing on the development of cognitive and thinking skills as a result of mediating mathematics to children aged 5-7. They found, that most of the new math curricula that focus on promoting mathematical thinking are based on the theories of both Piaget and Vygotsky, which emphasised the importance of integrating proper language through learning in order to better develop thinking skills. They focussed on the complexity of the language and the proper concepts used while mediating mathematical operations. Their study revealed not only that the children displayed better thinking skills in math classes during the year of the study, but also displayed better math performances and ability to learn independently two years later.

Nowadays, when information in all domains is easily available to all, educators need to focus on developing their students' thinking skills so they will be able to process and evaluate with and use the new knowledge. Lizarrga, Baquedano, and Oliver (2010) also claimed that today's younger generation needs more meticulous education in regard to the efficient use of their thinking skills, otherwise the knowledge they learn on their own will be wasted. Their study yielded two main conclusions: (1) as in other studies, teachers' *mediation* of the development of students' thinking skills promoted use of these skills when the students were dealing with new challenges; or (2) where the *mediation* integrated elements relating to the students' background, culture and environment, the effects of the *mediation* on the learners' cognitive development and use of the thinking skills were much more significant. In addition to the above conclusions, the teachers who participated in this study reported that they felt they had become better teachers as a result of their *mediation* to enhance their students' thinking development.

Developing updated curricula that all students can benefit from has been a challenge for educators for many years. This challenge is even greater when trying to develop curricula based on the learners' background and cognitive skills without knowing who the learners may be. Costa (2000) claimed that mediators, who practice mediating for better thinking development alongside integrating a variety of subject matter not only practice better *mediation* procedures, but also develop effective curricula that may be used for many years. While looking for evidence of thinking improvements as a result of *mediation*, Burden (2000) claimed that the results of effective *mediation* would be practiced in situations other than those in which the *mediation* was originally conducted. One of the core criteria of *mediation* is transferring knowledge and thinking principles from one situation to another, and therefore, the effective use of what was mediated may occur later in life.

Over the years, more educators accepted the significance of their role in developing better thinking skills among their learners. At the same time, many researchers also conducted studies to focus on the most effective way to succeed in promoting better cognitive and thinking development. Apparently, it seems that the most significant factor contributing to cognitive and thinking development is the people who mediate with the intention to develop these aspects. From this point of view, it is no longer a question of whether *mediation* can contribute to both cognitive and thinking development; it is now the time to learn how to better mediate with the intention to better develop these processes.

## 2.3. NECESSARY FOUNDATIONS FOR PRACTICING *MEDIATION*

Whereas the contribution of human *mediation* to people's cognitive development is accepted by many researchers of psychology, neurology and education, only few practitioners have developed practical models to implement *mediation*. In the first chapter, I presented six main approaches developed in different countries, by different researchers and at different periods, all in order to emphasise the consensus regarding the power society has over people's cognitive development. Some of the researchers also offered practical teaching models to allow better understanding of the cultural and social influences on cognitive development. Moreover, researchers agree that the powerful influence all societies have goes beyond daily routine activities (Flavian, 2017). From another perspective, researchers also emphasise that when educators or parents assess that a child does not present proper thinking processes, they can *mediate* in order to improve the child's cognitive development and thinking skills. As mentioned earlier, researchers also found that the main factor influencing efficient cognitive development was the mediator's intention to mediate specifically for effective use of thinking skills. The inquiry nowadays is to find effective and simple ways to promote *mediation* in schools.

From the theories presented in the first chapter, we can better develop a general perspective of the basic outlines for practicing *mediation*.

Piaget (2001), who defined three stages of cognitive development, emphasised the importance that one stage be well developed before continuing on to the next. At the same time, he also emphasised the role of the society in stimulating proper development. Therefore, when educators or any other caregivers identify a lack in a child's development, they should mediate using a learning activity specifically planned to help overcome that specific deficiency.

Vygotsky (Kozulin, 1999), who developed the model of cognitive development on the basis of the cultural interactions with surrounding people, named the learning and the cognitive development processes that developed as result of these interactions as the Zone of Proximal Development (ZPD), and provided outlines for practical *mediation*. Through his ZPD model, Vygotsky also emphasised and integrated the relations between effective learning interactions and language development. On the basis of the ZPD model, mediators can promote proper cognitive development as they trace the cultural interactions conducted in a specific situation, and provide appropriate *mediation*. Nevertheless, this is not a simple process and must be adjusted to suit every incidence of *mediation*. According to Vygotsky, in order to mediate effectively for learners' cognitive development, mediators must understand the cultural background of the learners and base their *mediation* on the perspective of that culture. In addition, mediators should learn and understand the uniqueness of the language used in order to integrate it through *mediation*. As for the significant differences between cultures and languages, from a practical perspective, teaching Vygotsky's approach through teacher-training programmes requires an intercultural teacher-training programme, which is a challenge in itself. In addition, even if a teacher has carefully studied Vygotsky's ZPD theory, the preparation for effective and practical *mediation* is complex and therefore this approach remains mainly theoretical. Nevertheless, the theory must be understood and mediators may use it as a basis for any preparation of practical *mediation*.

Both Piaget and Vygotsky wrote about the role of the society as the essential agent for thinking development through *mediation*. Nevertheless, conducting individual *mediation* in schools or in any other educational situations requires theoreticians to provide educators with more specific and practical information in regard to *mediation* and the variety of opportunities educators have to become mediators.

Gardner's theory can become useful for educators who wish to mediate for better thinking processes, as they plan their teaching-learning processes on the basis of the multiple intelligences approach. The practical meaning is that the study of any subject, theme, concept or other domain in school should be planned using a variety of processes that will contribute to the development of all seven intelligences among all learners. Although teaching according to the multiple intelligence theory seems to be the most effective method for all, researchers claim that there are various advantages and disadvantages in that approach as with any other learning theories (Batdi, 2017). Whereas the main advantages that teachers and researchers emphasise in regard to mediating on the basis of the multiple intelligences approach are the diverse experiences and opportunities they need to prepare in order to teach each topic, and the autonomy they have to choose learning activities, they also mention as disadvantages the difficulties in mediating all subjects from seven perspectives of intelligence, and in assessing learning according to this approach. The difficulties in assessing learning develop more from the desire to understand learners' thinking development as result of experiencing this type of learning. Because Gardner (2011) claims that educators are responsible for developing all thinking processes and all types of intelligences, the educators wish to follow those developments rather than assess knowledge as in the classic organisation of tests and grades. Therefore, before conducting any *mediation* on the basis of the multiple intelligences theory, planning of teaching and assessment should be carefully considered in order to ensure the integration of all intelligences throughout the entire process.

Feuerstein (2001) also developed structured approaches and models that present human *mediation* as a mandatory component in thinking development. But, unlike the other researchers and theoreticians, beyond the claim that thinking development cannot be conducted through direct exposure to stimuli and without *mediation*, he also developed a detailed *mediation* model to allow proper planning of *mediation* alongside tracing the mediatees' cognitive development.

Piaget's (2001) general learning model is known as the S → O → R model, which represents learning processes through which a Stimulus causes an Organism to develop a Response. Based on this model, Feuerstein (2001) added the mandatory human *mediation* that must be conducted between the Stimuli and the Organism, and after the Organism responds in order to provide proper feedback. The role of the mediator thus involves choosing the proper stimulus, planning the *mediation*, and then performing and assessing the process. Understanding that the goal of this *mediation* process is to promote thinking development, all *mediation* integrates two major elements: the cognitive functions throughout the input, elaboration and output stages, and the constructive process of *mediation*.

In addition to the general explanation of the concept of *mediation* and the explanations of the differences between *mediation* and teaching, Feuerstein divided the process into details that every educator can use to integrate *mediation* into all types of learning situations in schools. In addition, from the perspective that each child should eventually integrate into society, Feuerstein also referred to the fact that *mediation* should be conducted in both individual and group learning. His emphasis was that all *mediation* must initially be relevant to the individual but also to include the relevance of the future as the individuals become independent social members of their society (Reichenberg & Rand, 2000).

According to Feuerstein's Mediated Learning Experience (MLE) approach, the practice of *mediation* is based on
several stages. The first refers to the mediatee: the mediator should learn about the mediatee's background in order
to better adjust the *mediation* process. Although the role of
social *mediation* is significant, *mediation* must be conducted
according to learners' cultural and cognitive characteristics.
Thus, even if children grow up in the same environment and
share similar experiences, their learning and cognitive function development may differ (Feuerstein et al., 2006).

In the next stage, the mediator analyses the information
using the thinking skills and the list of cognitive functions
throughout the input, elaboration and output phases, as the
criteria for organising the information. Only then, when the
mediator better understand the strengths of the mediatees'
thinking processes and those, which need to be better, mediated, can the planning of the *mediation* begin.

Planning *mediation* according to the MLE also requires
choosing a domain that relates to the mediatees' culture,
background, interest or in any other way. *Mediation* cannot be conducted theoretically; it must be integrated into
the learning activities. The final stage of planning refers to
the *mediation* criteria that Feuerstein (2001) defined. His 12
parameters of *mediation* allow better planning and assessment, even though not every mediated interaction will involve
all of them. Despite the essential flexibility of the *mediation*
process in according with the mediators' understanding of
the mediatees' needs, at least the first three parameters must
always be included.

Feuerstein organised his 12 parameters of *mediation* into
two sub-groups to allow mediators to better choose the most
essential parameters to use: three universal parameters and
nine situational parameters. The 12 parameters are organised
as described below (Feuerstein et al., 2002).

### 2.3.1. Feuerstein's Universal Parameters of *Mediation*

According to Feuerstein's MLE the core of all mediational processes is the existence of the three universal parameters: intentionality and reciprocity, transcendence and meaning. These must be implemented throughout the interaction in order for it to qualify as a *mediation* process.

(1) *Intentionality and reciprocity*: Every *mediation* begins with the mediator's intention to modify the mediatee's cognitive and thinking skills, through planned interaction. The role of the mediator is to orient the nature of the interaction with the stimuli by focussing on shaping thinking processes. The mediator's intention can be practiced only with mediatee reciprocity, that is, the mediatee's responsiveness needs and awareness. This first parameter of *mediation* presents the intent of each participant to take part in the learning and changing by bringing their experiences and insights to make it significant for all, as well as transferrable beyond the specific situation.

(2) *Mediation for transcendence*: Transcendence is defined as the widening of the core of learning beyond the immediate situation and the specific context in which it was acquired. Mediating for transcendence occurs when the mediator broadens the opportunities to learn from a specific and concrete situation. Through such *mediation*, the mediatees consistently enlarge their cognitive and emotional repertoire, and learn to look for new opportunities to apply what they have learned.

(3) *Mediation of meaning*: Although the MLE seeks to modify cognitive abilities, *mediation* of meaning is the emotional, affective component of the interaction. Through *mediation*

of meaning the mediators enable efficient delivery of the core context of learning to the most relevant area for the mediatees, and by doing so, the intrinsic motivation for reciprocity towards cognitive modifiability is increased. This process, conducted alongside transcendence, can increase the mediatees' cognitive modifiability.

## 2.3.2. Situational Parameters Reinforcing and Elaborating MLE

In addition to the above mandatory three parameters, nine different parameters may be integrated according to the situation in order to cater to particular needs of the mediatees. These parameters are mediated differently, depending on differences in culture and life situation. From the MLE perspective, each of the nine parameters can be mediated only in addition to the first three universal ones described above.

(4) *Mediation of the feelings of competence*: Competence in general and specifically the feeling of competence, are the key features of cognitive, emotional and behavioural functioning and coping with challenges. Competence is related to motivation, specifically in situations where individuals are required to achieve better than they are used to. Because the feeling of competence is not the direct outcome of the perception of one's real ability, there is a need for intervention and *mediation* by a social agent. The role of the mediator in these situations is to translate the individual's performance in a way that the individual will better understand the results of his/her behaviour and will develop appropriate awareness of it to improve coping with similar situations in the future.

(5) *Mediation of regulation and control of behaviour*: Regulation and control of behaviour accelerate the

individual's orientation towards self-reflection, and provides the necessary feedback for decision making in the future. Moreover, *mediation* of regulation and control of behaviour creates the cognitive prerequisites to enhance the individuals' ability to adopt and use new modes of behaviour.

(6) *Mediation of sharing behaviour*: Becoming a member of a society requires willingness to reach out from the 'self' towards participating with others, and at the same time to allow others to participate in one's thinking and emotional processes. Although observing this type of behaviour is possible from a young age, the results of mediating for sharing behaviour may appear only after a long period of time because of the complex influences of both cultural and psychological factors.

(7) *Mediation of individuation and psychological differentiation*: On the basis of enhancing the *mediation* of sharing behaviour and the sense of competence, children can learn to feel secure in their environment. At this stage they are ready for the *mediation* of psychological differentiation, which enhances their self-perception as separated, articulated and independent entities. This is also mediated alongside the *mediation* of belonging (see below).

(8) *Mediation of goal seeking, goal setting and goal-achieving behaviour*: The processes of seeking a goal in any area of life and striving towards it are based on both a high modality of thinking skills and one's competence to be able to change reality. Mediating the need to search and choose goals is a process in which mediators enrich and articulate mediatees' lives as learning entities. This process also includes *mediation* for better organisation and use of core principles of learning.

(9)   *Mediation of challenge: the search for novelty and complexity:* Challenging behaviour to change, to be modified with the mediatee's consent and control, is one of the most important goals educators should be aware of. Mediators at this stage focus on the ability to confront rather than avoid novel and complex challenges, leading mediatees to become aware of the challenges they face and what they might face in the future.

(10)  *Mediation of awareness of the human being as a changing entity:* This parameter of *mediation* presents the core of belief in cognitive modifiability. At this stage, mediators need to mediate to the individual and to society that modifiability is a uniquely human feature that allows adaptation and flexibility through learning. Mediators should look for signs of change among their mediatees, and make them aware of how they have changed in order to help them make other changes on their own in the future.

(11)  *Mediation of the search for an optimistic alternatives:* *Mediation* of an optimistic alternative through learning has an impact on the cognitive structure and modifiability of the individual's behaviour. While a pessimistic point of view of problems causes a passive-acceptant approach, an optimistic point of view motivates for dynamic, active and creative approaches. Mediating children for positive outcomes causes them to continue to act that way independently later on in life.

(12)  *Mediation of the feeling of belonging:* People's readiness to broaden their views beyond the immediacy of their own experiences depends on their feeling of belonging to the society in which they live. *Mediating*

of the feeling of belonging includes all the parameters of *mediation*, but mostly serves as an integrational link that strengthens transcendence and gives perspective to the regulation of behaviour.

Whereas education processes integrate a variety of theories and approaches, through this chapter I have clarified the commonalities and differences between teaching- learning and mediating. There is no doubt as to the importance of both processes: teaching and mediating, but it is also obvious that effective teaching may be developed and conducted when it derives from the perspective of *mediation*. Some key possibilities for *mediation* are presented in Chapter 4, with a focus on the MLE approach based on Feuerstein's theory of cognitive modifiability. The 12 parameters of *mediation* explained at the end of this chapter clarify for educators the aspects and the parameters of *mediation* they need to consider as they plan and practice *mediation* situations to promote cognitive modifiability among their learners. Although the theory of MLE was developed by Feuerstein already early in the 1970s, only lately researchers began examine its efficiency. In those studies they claim to find that learning of new knowledge is much more efficient while it conducted on a basis of organised processes with clear meaning of the goals. Beyond the basic learning, organisation and understanding of the goals contribute to better use of the information in the future by transcending it to new situations (Brod, Lindenberger, Wanger, & Shing, 2016).

*Mediation* can and should be practiced through a variety of procedures planned according to the mediatees' characteristics. The following chapters refer to the core characteristics of our mediatees along with examples of ways to implement *mediation* in schools and in life.

# 3

# SCHOOL STUDENTS; LEARNING DIFFERENTIATIONS TEACHERS NEED TO RECOGNISE

The role of schools, which were originally developed to transfer necessary knowledge through planned and organised processes in order to better prepare children for life, has not significantly changed to this day. Nevertheless, factors such as the dynamic changes and development of society, the variety of students growing up in different cultures and attending the same schools, and the amount of knowledge that has accumulated have rendered the main goal of school so complex as to be almost unachievable. As early as the start of the twentieth century, Dewey (1938/2015) claimed there were no similarities between the organisation or goals of school on the one hand, and society on the other, and that most school curricula had little or no relevance to learners' future needs. He thus recommended radically changing the goals of schooling and the teaching methodologies used to achieve them.

From this perspective, nowadays the main goal for all educators should focus on developing learners' thinking skills to allow them to deal with situations in life independently.

In no way am I suggesting that we should ignore the importance of teaching knowledge in schools. I believe that teachers' knowledge and expertise in a certain domain must be used to stimulate learners' thinking development and not vice versa. In our world, whereas most of the information is available for most learners, only educators who mediate for thinking development can help their pupils become independent learners and thinkers, able to turn available information into useful knowledge. Moreover, promoting the importance of learning specific domains that will allow learners better inclusion in their society in the future has elevated the need for professional teachers who are also experts in certain domains of knowledge. In this chapter, I will present key issues pertaining to learning differentiation that mediators need to be aware of, which will be followed in the next chapter by practical examples of well-planned *mediation* based on these understandings.

Understanding the complexity teachers face while aiming to pass on their knowledge to all their learners, encouraged many theoreticians to develop the field of pedagogy, along with developing different models of taxonomies that present the levels of learners' thinking development. Towards the end of this chapter, some theoretical review of pedagogy, taxonomy and thinking development is presented as well.

The massive development of schools around the world in terms of the number of schools, class size and new goals for education, also leads educators to refer to their students as groups of learners rather than as individual learners who study in groups. This is despite the fact that educators understand that learning processes differ from learner to learner for a variety of criteria such as age, culture, cognitive ability, etc. Some differences between learners are recognised by the teachers as they begin to teach, either because of their visibility or because the teachers were informed about them beforehand. However, many such differences can only be diagnosed through teaching-learning activities and only when teachers actively look for them. In order to develop efficient *mediation* processes that are based on teaching-learning interactions, educators must understand the meaning of differentiation among students' learning processes. Although there are general definitions that emphasise differentiation among students according to their cognitive abilities, emotional stability and availability to learn, or other challenges, most educators are not trained to use these definitions of differentiation effectively when planning learning opportunities.

One of the reasons educators struggle with planning proper learning activities for learners assessed with any type of learning difficulty is the fact that learning, cognitive and thinking assessments are conducted by professionals other than educators who use a different vocabulary to describe learning skills. While such assessments are only conducted by psychologists, it is the educators who are responsible for developing appropriate learning activities on the basis of the official curricula for those learners. Moreover, in most cases, educators are not involved in the procedures of assessing the type of learning difficulty of their students, even though they are expected to apply the ensuing recommendations to daily learning activities in school; a process that is often neither simple nor obvious. Understanding how our brain functions is one strategy educators use to better understand the meaning of learning, but this is not enough. The solution for this language gap between different professionals offered through this book is the approach of *mediation* rather than teaching. When focussing on the goal of developing better thinking processes, mediators plan their mediating activities on the basis of understanding the challenges learners are facing rather than using definitions that describe their difficulties. Understanding differentiation is the path to creating efficient *mediation* processes that allow learners become independent thinkers. Moreover, mediators should focus on two main strategies: (a) understanding the possible reasons for the lack of learning, and (b) looking for new *mediation* interactions that will allow thinking development.

Following the theories and studies presented earlier, educators and adults in general may become powerful mediators who take advantage of brain modifiability to enhance thinking and learning processes. By accepting the role of mediator, educators also accept their responsibility to look for suitable *mediation* processes that promote learning among all their students.

The endless list of concepts used to describe differentiation among learners may be divided into two main categories that are explained in detail along a continuum of motivation as a core parameter for learning and thinking development, and cultural differences that cause differentiation in thinking development. From this perspective, educators should avoid referring to all pupils as one homogenous group, and look for the unique *mediation* each learner needs in order to develop better thinking processes and become an independent learner.

## 3.1. MOTIVATION, LEARNING AND THINKING DEVELOPMENT

Motivation is an abstract theoretical concept that has been defined by several researchers as the internal energy that leads one's actions towards achieving a goal (Cook & Artino, 2016). Although countless theories and scholars have offered different explanations as to what drives human motivation, the only one agreed and accepted view is that without it people will not make the effort to cope with any challenge. Hadwin (2008) emphasises that while researchers find it hard to define the core of the concept, they all agree that motivation is a critical and essential factor all learners need to promote efficient learning. Beyond the consensus that motivation is subjective and therefore differs among individuals, there is also consensus that motivation is stimulated by both extrinsic and intrinsic factors (Pink, 2009). The differentiation between the source of the stimulation is not relevant when looking at long-term learning, because even when the initial stimulation is driven by extrinsic factors, the motivation continuum will be developed from intrinsic sources that differ from one person to another.

Cook and Artino (2016) claimed that while the general correlation between success in learning and motivation is almost taken for granted, some researchers also look for additional aspects that relate to this correlation. For example, social-cognitive theoreticians stress self-efficacy as the most important factor driving people's motivation. From the perspective of goal-orientation theory, researchers claim that learners tend to engage in tasks according to their understanding of their mastery of the topic or their chances of succeeding.

One of the assumptions many educators base their teaching on is that learners who are interested in what they are studying will be motivated to make the effort to learn. Moreover, some educators consider intrinsic motivation to learn to be a natural trait all people are born with and, as a result, take children's learning for granted and find it difficult to accept situations in which children are no longer interested in learning. Although the basic assumption is correct, the process of promoting motivation is complex and includes a variety of factors (Maslow, 2014). The reciprocal influences of motivation and other factors in relation to learning and thinking development have led many researchers to better understand how to motivate learners to cope with cognitive challenges. Pink (2009), one of the researchers who believes that all people should find the secret key that drives their motivation to deal with challenges, focusses on the sense of satisfaction as the most effective factor. Even when the motivational factor is extrinsic, the feeling of satisfaction is intrinsic and individual, and this feeling recharges motivations for all situations.

Research on the core of motivation to deal with a high level of academic challenges led to the conclusion that learners' understanding of the meaning of the task increases their motivation to cope with it (Davis, Kelley, Kim, Tang, & Hicks, 2016). These researchers also emphasised that when learners do not have a specific goal or a clear perception of the meaning of the task, they may complete the task correctly but will not put in extra effort and will not try to use what they have learned elsewhere. From another perspective, Hadwin (2008) analysed the connections between self-regulation and motivation. He argued that both the motivation to succeed and knowledge about the task influence self-regulation, and that this process may become circular. In other words, the more motivated the learners are, the better the strategies they choose and the better they regulate their actions in order to succeed. Also, the more experience of success they have, the higher their motivation to regulate their work becomes.

Educators who understand the reciprocal influences of motivation and coping with challenges through learning should base their teaching on these factors while promoting thinking development. Nevertheless, they must also understand that lack of motivation blocks learners' learning and thinking development (Maslow, 2014). From this perspective, the mediators' role as the agents responsible for thinking development, learning and better socialisation also includes the responsibility to increase motivation for coping with cognitive challenges as a basis for all other learning processes. Thus, when children do not show any interest in learning, mediators should look for the source of this lack and focus their *mediation* towards the goal of renewing intrinsic motivation for learning.

Although the search for the reason for the lack of motivation seems complex, there are, in fact, simple ways to find the answers. Educators must bear in mind that although different learners in the same classroom may have different reasons for their lack of motivation (Maslow, 2014), causing learners to become motivated is the key to continuing the *mediation* processes towards better thinking development.

For example, when children display no interest in learning, or express no motivation to cope with learning, mediators can ask themselves, their colleagues and their learners some simple questions such as: Does this lack of motivation derive from a lack of success? lack of interest in the subject matter? lack of thinking skills? or, lack of social interactions that allow understanding of the meaning of learning? Answers to these and other similar questions provide mediators with the information they need to understand what is blocking learners' essential motivation to cope with cognitive challenges, and plan proper *mediation* processes to re-motivate them.

Integrating some of the motivational theories of learning mentioned above make it possible to compose an approach that seeks the motivational key of our learners, along with *mediation* for the meaning of learning and coping with cognitive challenges, not only to promote efficient learning in general, but mainly to promote efficient thinking development.

## 3.2. CULTURE, LEARNING AND THINKING DEVELOPMENT

Several scholars and theoreticians refer to culture as a significant factor that influences thinking development. This notion reoccurred throughout the review of the main theories and approaches towards thinking development in the first chapter of this book. While Dewey argued that society was responsible for every learner's intrinsic motivation to learn and hence that society influences all learners' thinking development, Piaget and Vygotsky claimed that the direct and indirect activities to which society chooses to expose learners are the triggers for learners' thinking development. From a different point of view of society's role in learners' thinking development, Feuerstein argued that not only is society responsible for proper thinking development, it is also responsible for finding ways to remedy any lack in thinking development that learners may present via *mediation*. Gardner explained the role of society in developing learners' thinking processes by defining a number of thinking processes people are born with and may therefore use, and called them 'intelligences'. Emphasising that although learners are born with a basic ability to use all types of intelligences, they may display their use of one main intelligence through most of their learning activities, but then it is up to the society to challenge them by exposing them to the additional thinking processes they may also use.

Analysing the variety of factors that link people's thinking development, learning processes and their culture, leads researchers to focus mainly on the language people use (Flavian & Dan, 2018). From studies that focussed on immigrants' learning processes, researchers concluded that all languages represent the cultural codes, structures, norms and attitudes that influence people thinking processes on a daily basis (Kozulin, 2000). Moreover, the processes of organising thoughts and feelings into words so others will understand the core meaning and will communicate accordingly are complex and depend on cultural norms. Following learning and integration processes among immigrants and minorities also led researchers to the conclusion that language is the main challenge they face. Their explanation is based on the fact that because of their deficiencies in the main spoken language used in schools, their achievements are lower than their peers and as a result, their teachers expect less from them and mediate with less belief in their ability to change cognitively (Feuerstein, 2002). The lack of belief in their ability to cognitively change, causes for lack in the entire learning process they go through, and only proper *mediation* by people who recognise their culture can promote learning and thinking development (Feuerstein et al., 2006; Kozulin, 2000). The relations between language, *mediation* and thinking development were also studied among children with Down Syndrome (DS) who studied in schools (Aloni & Kozulin, 2015). Whereas children with DS face seriously challenges, educators tend to use low level of language and without making any effort to develop their thinking skills from the perspective that it would be frustrated and useless. During their study, Aloni and Kozulin trained teachers to mediate language skills and thinking process according to Feuerstein's *mediation* approach. The results of their study strongly support the shared perspective of many researchers, that by proper *mediation* both language and thinking skills are improved and there is a reciprocal influence between the two domains. Another conclusion researchers share from these studies is, that conducting proper communication according to the rules of grammar and syntax of a certain language alongside referring to cultural norms, promotes high level of thinking development and better results of learning processes (Gardner, 2011).

Neuroscientists who focus on their studies on the roles of executive functions through thinking development also support the approach that human intervention may modify brain functions through efficient intervention (Moyer, 2014). Throughout their studies, they have developed the domain of neuropedagogy, and specifically examined the influence of culture, social interactions and organised teaching on human thinking development from other points of view. Their main conclusion, based on a variety of studies, emphasises that the brain generally changes as a result of all types of interactions with the environment. While focussing on planned mediated interactions, they conclude that brain functions can be better developed and changed after specific and planned learning interactions (Barkely, 2012; Friedman, Grobgeld, & Teichman-Weinberg, 2019).

Integrating the three areas of culture, learning and thinking development seems to be more complex than one might think. Whereas most educators are familiar with the above perception and they understand that society, environment and culture influence one's thinking development, they hardly refer to this factor when preparing learning activities or learning assessments in schools. Moreover, educators are hardly aware of the fact that the school environment is a sub-culture of society and thus school culture influences learners' thinking development as well. Practically, based on the above and on Feuerstein's theory, the main assumption that should serve as the basis for all educators' teaching plans is that no matter what thinking processes learners use when they enter school, educators can modify end enhance them for all their students.

Beyond the theoretical approach that both culture and environment influence thinking development there are other practical factors educators can refer to while planning and practicing learning and mediated interactions. Recognising culture as one of the main factors that influences learners' thinking development also serves as a solid basis to understand the core of the differences among them. Educators thus need to learn the outlines of each culture learners came from and conclude what the structure of their thinking processes might be. Although it might seem almost impossible to learn about everyone's culture, once the educator has learned and understood the role of certain important core criteria for thinking development, their efficiency in promoting learners' thinking development will increase. One of the main cultural characteristics that educators are familiar with is language. Unlike what many people think, the role of language goes far beyond communication among people. Two of the main uses that proper knowledge of language allow are independent learning and the development of self-expression. First, language is the basis for learning in all areas of life and with proper use of language, learners can become independent investigators of any area they may be interested in. In addition, learners may develop proper linguistic skills to express their knowledge, thoughts and feelings. These two uses also promote learners who better integrate into society, which is the goal of education in general. Because mediating in general and specifically teaching in schools are two types of learning interactions that are based on language, educators refer to language as an obvious skill everyone learns automatically, unless the learners have been assessed with a disability that affects language development. Considering language development as an automatic process causes educators to ignore learners' cultural uniqueness along with promoting the development of linguistic intelligence (Gardner, 2011), and the lack of those processes directly prevents proper *mediation* of thinking development.

Over the last 60 years researchers have conducted a variety of studies to better understand how vocabulary and well-structured language influence the development of thinking. Their main goal is to use this understanding while planning teacher-training programmes and different curricula for disciplines studied in school (Flavian and Dan, 2018). When such studies began, Draper and Moeller (1971) focussed on studying the influences of vocabulary on academic achievements. Their main conclusion was that a rich vocabulary increases students' academic achievements. But, they also emphasised that understanding the meaning of each word, the possible uses of the vocabulary in the different domains they study in schools, and understanding the structure of the language while expressing their knowledge were also significant factors in increasing academic achievements.

## 3.3. PEDAGOGY, TAXONOMY AND TEACHING STRATEGIES

Understanding the meaning of learning along with understanding the variety of opportunities people have to learn throughout their life were the two main factors that motivated the development of a domain that will serve as a structured, professional and scientific basis for conducting proper and efficient teaching-learning processes. Many scholars, educators and theoreticians have contributed to the foundation of the development of pedagogy. Looking back at the history of studies on teaching-learning, Vygotsky (Daniels, 2016) was the first person to officially integrate educational processes with psychological perspectives and human activities. This scientific integration is actually the unique art of education and the basis of pedagogy. Although all who are involved with education claim to understand what pedagogy includes, the definition of the term is very abstract. Fischer (1998) explained that pedagogy addresses the processes of creations, discussions, exchanging information and transformation of consciousness that take place in the interactions of three agencies: teachers, learners and the knowledge they produce together. Freeman and Karlsson (2012) refer to pedagogy as a professional teaching framework that allows educators to understand and plan learning processes while considering the group of learning and whole child along while relating to curricula standards, making accommodations for differences in children's cultures, languages, individual characteristics, abilities and disabilities. Over the years, the role of pedagogy became more significant as educators sought to better teach specific knowledge through a process that would allow learners to enhance and use it in the future. For example, Rudolph (2008) described a process of over 15 years that was focussed on the development of science education as a unique domain and what the best pedagogical approach would be when teaching science. Realising that education exists in public areas other than schools, the field of public pedagogy developed as well, in order to allow learners everywhere to engage in lifelong learning (Hickling-Hudson & Hepple, 2015).

Whereas researching the field of teaching methods in order to develop practical pedagogical perspectives also led to the accumulation of an enormous amount of important knowledge, educators found it hard to put into practice. Learning from the field of biology how the biologists created a taxonomy to classify and categorise all species and other relevant factors, Bloom (1956) created a learning taxonomy to allow educators to better understand the processes of thinking and learning among their learners, and at the same time to provide educators with a practical tool to develop proper curricula in all domains. Moreover, Bloom encouraged educators to use this taxonomy in order to create thinkers as opposed to students who simply memorise and recall information. To facilitate implementation of this taxonomy, Bloom defined six levels to classify and organise the order of learning, from a basic level of knowledge to the highest level of using the new knowledge. Accordingly, each stage is a prerequisite for the following one, as the taxonomy is organised from lower- to higher-order thinking skills. Whereas each level is sophisticated, it also designs possibilities to transcend specific subject matter along with encouraging the operation of different cognitive skills that suit individuals within a group of learners (Scully, 2017). The six stages of Bloom's taxonomy are as follows:

(1) *Knowledge*: the basic information and data the learners need to learn in order to construct a solid basis for future learning processes. This stage also includes observation and recall of information, knowledge of dates, events, places, major ideas and mastery of subject matter. At this stage of thinking, learners may recall or recognise the knowledge, without necessarily having the ability to apply this knowledge.

(2) *Comprehension*: this stage is important to make sure learners undergo the process of understanding the information. Learners need to be able to interpret the facts, describe and explain the new knowledge. They are expected to present their understanding of the core meaning of the knowledge studied, to translate knowledge into new contexts, to interpret facts, to compare, to contrast, to order, to group, to infer causes and to predict consequences.

(3) *Application*: At this stage learners have to actually apply, or use, the knowledge they have learned. They also need to solve or examine new problems, yet structurally similar, with the information they have gained and with proper use of concepts.

(4) *Analysis*: At this level, learners are required to go beyond the basic knowledge they have acquired, and use the relevant factors to analyse new problems. On the basis of the three previous stages, learners are expected to recognise the patterns of the new subject matter, to organise the information, to identify the hidden meanings and to detect the new components in order to solve the new challenge.

(5) *Synthesis*: Throughout the stage of synthesis, it is
    essential that learners use given facts to organise and
    create new knowledge or to predict a solution of a new
    problem. They are also expected to integrate knowledge
    from multiple subjects and synthesise the information
    before presenting a conclusion. Learners may use old
    ideas to create new ones; they may generalise from given
    facts, relate to knowledge from several areas, predict, or
    draw a conclusion.

(6) *Evaluation*: This is the highest stage of thinking
    according to Bloom's taxonomy. At this stage, learners
    are expected to assess information and to come to
    a conclusion they can explain rationally. In order to
    succeed at this level, learners must go through all the
    previous five stages of learning and thinking. Then,
    they need to compare and discriminate between ideas;
    they need to assess and critique the value of theories,
    facts and ideas. Learners need to make choices based on
    reasoned arguments and recognise the subjectivity
    of ideas.

Based on Bloom's taxonomy as summarised above, theoreticians and researchers have developed additional thinking
taxonomies. Nevertheless, I chose to present the original one,
since many educators use it even today. Moreover, this taxonomy is very simple to implement as I will present in the
next chapter.

Pedagogy, as defined above, is the field that integrates
between the teachers, the subject matter and the learners.
Whereas pedagogy offers educators perspectives for learning
and teaching, and the taxonomy offers a hierarchic perspective
of thinking stages learners need to experience, at school teachers are expected to efficiently integrate all these theories and
models with the subject matter they teach. Translating abstract

theories and models into practice is the talent of teaching, and there is no single way to do so. On the basis of their culture, language and training, teachers are required to use different teaching strategies in order to make sure all learners achieve the goals. The processes of choosing efficient teaching strategies are complex and dynamic, where one strategy may be efficient for one group of learners but not for others, or, may be efficient for teaching at one level of the taxonomy but not for another. Therefore, the overall teaching strategy that this book offers is the *mediation* approach, as it can be adapted to a variety of learners who study in one group, to their culture, and to the content teachers wish to teach.

Mediators who wish to promote thinking development among their mediatees need to recognise the unique cognitive abilities each of them has, along with understanding the reasons for the differences between them. The search for the causes of the differences among learners can prepare a solid ground for planning and conducting efficient mediated interactions. Nevertheless, it is important to remember that following and assessing efficient *mediation* is neither a simple nor a short process. Thus, true and efficient mediated interactions can be assessed only when mediatees independently and properly use the core of what they have experienced in new learning and challenging situations that usually occur when the mediator is not around.

Mediators who plan mediated interactions in school should also recognise the field of pedagogy along with taxonomy of thinking, in order to develop a proper learning environment that integrates as many factors as possible to influence mediatees' learning and thinking processes.

In this chapter, I focussed on motivation, cultural and language differences as the main criteria for understanding the differences among learners while planning mediating for thinking development. From my perspective, these parameters include all other criteria for differentiation among learners. Nowadays, when some learners do not meet the academic goals as well as their classmates do, it is accepted that educators will ask professional psychologists to assess their thinking skills according to some official psychological assessment. But, although such assessments may lead to proper definitions of the learning difficulties, it does not provide educators with any practical perspective of how promote better *mediation* to enhance learners' thinking development. From the perspective of *mediation* as the path to successful thinking development, mediators should focus on understanding the challenges learners need to face along with understanding the causes of what is preventing them from learning, rather than trying to define the difficulties. Moreover, by focussing on how to overcome the challenges, mediators also present their belief in mediatees' ability to change cognitively and thereby they can increase their mediatees' motivation to cope with learning challenges.

# 4

## *MEDIATION* AND TEACHING FOR STUDENTS' THINKING DEVELOPMENT

Throughout the previous chapters, the concepts of *mediation* and thinking development were examined from different points of view by presenting different theories, alongside a look at the role of society in the development of learners' cognitive development. In addition, the domain of neuro-pedagogy was described to emphasise the mutual influences researchers have found between learning processes and brain development. Integrating the core ideas of learning theories with updated brain study findings highlights *mediation*'s contribution to thinking development. Whereas educators, parents, therapists and other caregivers may learn those theories and approaches in a variety of academic programmes, putting the theories into practice requires much more than theoretical learning. Integrating all the previously mentioned theories and approaches to create a practical path, reveals one parameter they all share; the ability to promote human brain function. Both theoreticians and researchers claim that motivating our mind to deal with cognitive challenges not only improves thinking processes in theory but actually changes the way our brain works (Pink, 2009) so that mediators' efforts may remain with us for life.

This chapter takes the readers through the process of converting theory into practice, by demonstrating examples of *mediation*. After presenting an integrated model for planning thinking development through *mediation*, this chapter aims to demonstrate the use of the entire model to prepare mediated interactions at school as well as ones that can be practiced at home on a daily basis, with children younger than school age. The goal is to allow a variety of caregivers to practice *mediation* for thinking development and make it an integral part of communication in their lives. I have chosen typical situations, but it is important to remember that these are only examples. It is up to the caregivers to modify the suggested *mediation* goals and processes according to the children's needs and to the culture in which they are growing up. These situations present the power of *mediation* in developing one's understanding and thinking in ways that not only solve a social situation but also provide cognitive tools to deal independently with similar situations later on in life.

Following the examples for *mediation* through family interactions, I will focus on ways to plan and conduct school lessons based on the *mediation* approach. In this context, in addition to the basic integrative *mediation* model, I will also refer to the concepts of pedagogy and taxonomy previously explained in Chapter 3. The references to Feuerstein's MLE theory will include the 27 cognitive functions through the three stages of thinking (input, elaboration and output), while the references to Bloom's taxonomy will help plan thinking challenges, along with integrating improvement of cognitive functions. Educators who follow the rationale behind the division of the examples of *mediation* in these two sub-chapters will be able to better mediate for transcendence and plan *mediation* for a wider range of possibilities.

As explained in detail in Chapter 3, while pedagogy developed to help train better teachers around the world, different philosophers, psychologists and educators developed theories of pedagogy according to their perspective of the field. The various pedagogical approaches integrate two main concepts: teaching and learning. However, while those concepts usually relate to specific subject matter, adding the notion of *mediation* makes the process meaningful and effective for lifelong learning due to the focus on helping everyone become independent learners.

Another criterion that highlights the difference between mediating at home and at school relates to the opportunities mediators have to plan mediated interactions. While mediated interactions between children and their caregivers occur on a daily basis and are frequently spontaneous, educators usually have the time to plan their mediated interaction in relation to a specific discipline they teach in schools. Regardless of these differences, through all mediated interaction the mediators should motivate mediatees to cope independently with new learning situations by acquiring the effective thinking skills they need.

One additional step before putting *mediation* theories into practice is to remember that these theories were initially developed out of a criticism of society for not putting enough effort into developing children's' thinking skills, and it was only years later that *mediation* was viewed as an essential tool for educational processes in schools. Hence, while we expect mediated activities in school to be carried out by teachers, it is highly desirable for all caregivers to conduct mediated processes on a daily basis, as was originally intended; one doesn't have to be a formal educator of a specific discipline in order to be an excellent and efficient mediator for all kind of life situations. Stressing this perspective further, every mediated interaction should refer both to school materials and to daily life activities.

## 4.1. AN INTEGRATED MODEL FOR PLANNING THINKING DEVELOPMENT THROUGH *MEDIATION*

The explanation of the meaning of *mediation* in Chapter 2 emphasised that planning a mediated process is a prerequisite for promoting efficient interactions between mediator and mediatee that will lead towards thinking development and independent thinking. Nowadays, many teaching models have been developed to generate organised learning processes. Whereas those teaching models focus on how to better teach a specific subject within a specific discipline, the model I present here was developed in order to better plan *mediation* for thinking development, a *mediation* process that will motivate independent thinkers alongside the acquisition of new knowledge. As presented previously in this book, several theoreticians have referred to *mediation* as a general process that must be integrated into learning and thinking development. Consequently, educators find it hard to select one approach over another and often claim that planning and implementing efficient *mediation* is too confusing. To make this process simpler, and without undermining the contribution of any learning theory, the planning of mediated interactions offered in this chapter are based mainly on Feuerstein's theory; the 12 parameters of *mediation* and the use of the defined cognitive functions. These clear parameters allow mediators to plan and to follow the consequences of the process. Nevertheless, since the success of *mediation* relies on a delicate integration of approaches, the other approaches presented previously in this book in regard to the meaning of *mediation*, learning and pedagogy, are integrated within the model as well.

From the core perspective of the role of *mediation*, the following model is a basis for planning and adapting learning processes according to mediatees' needs, while it is only later that the mediators' goals are defined. But, while we plan and later implement our mediated interactions, we must keep in mind that results may not turn out as we planned, because of several parameters that we cannot predict and consider ahead of time. Moyes (2014) stresses this perception in regard to the role of planning teaching-learning interactions and the need to be flexible while carrying them out, by claiming that 'if they can't learn the way we teach, maybe we should teach the way they learn' (p. 117). Therefore, efficient planning can only be used as a solid basis for logical changing and adapting of processes.

This model aims to provide mediators with the opportunity to develop thinking among all mediatees through all domains of life. Accordingly, all mediated interaction should include four main phases: (a) collecting data about the mediatees, (b) defining the goal of the mediated interaction, (c) planning the mediated interaction according to a stable scheme alongside a focus on relevant thinking processes and (d) reflecting on the process. Each phase is the basis for the next, while the fourth should be used in conjunction with any other source of data for the first phase and not the end of the process.

*Data collection:* Achieving any type of goal demands an efficient process of collecting relevant data, but defining goals and collecting data are circular processes that need to be carefully managed. Whereas relevant data can be collected only after a general goal is defined, in order to define a general goal, basic data must be collected as well.

The overall goal that will guide mediators using this integrated model I offer is: 'to promote efficient thinking development through *mediation*'. Therefore, all the relevant data should contribute to the attainment of this goal.

While collecting relevant data, mediators should consider the following basic information:

(1) *Who are the mediatees?*

   While it seems to be obvious to know the age and gender of the mediatees, it is important that mediators make sure they know precise information other than only that. Knowing the exact age of the mediatees is important for better understanding of the thinking, motor and social skills they expect to be used in comparison to the society the children live in, and accordingly to assess what cognitive functions should be more mediated. Gender, on the other hand, relates more specifically to the culture of the mediatees, and in multicultural societies this parameter is significant. Mediators need to recognise and understand mediatees' cultural roots and norms in order to efficiently use Feuerstein's three universal parameters of *mediation*: intentionality and reciprocity, transcendence and meaning. In reference to culture, it is essential to know whether the mediatees were born in the current learning area, what their mother-tongue is, and how well they understand and use the language the mediators use.

Since the overall goal is to promote thinking development among mediatees, the mediators must also look for information about how efficiently the mediatees use their cognitive functions, what their strengths are and which functions might need to be more mediated. In addition, mediators should be awareness of mediatees' previous knowledge of the content around which the *mediation* is to be conducted, and base learning processes accordingly. Whereas information about age, gender and language are usually simple to collect, information about thinking skills and previous knowledge is dynamic and changes from one interaction to another. This means that after each mediated interaction mediators must update their information about the mediatees and base their subsequent planning only on the updated data.

(2)  *Who are the mediators?*

Knowing yourself as a mediator wishing to promote thinking development is an essential stage of the *mediation*. Within the general self-knowledge, researchers point out the importance of developing realistic self-awareness, which is part of the processes Feuerstein defined as *mediation* for competence and individuation and psychological differentiation (for details, see Chapter 2). Borg (2001) stressed that teachers' realistic awareness of the content they need to teach alongside their awareness of their teaching skills are the main factors to conduct efficient teaching processes. Nevertheless, this basis increases their feel of confident to deal with problems that their students bring up, and therefore they deal with those questions more effectively. The integration of all above contributes to teachers' ability to develop better teaching programmes, moreover their ability to develop mediated interactions. . From this perspective, mediators must better recognise themselves as mediators, their understanding elements and processes of *mediation* and their knowledge of the topic on which they are going to base their *mediation* processes. In addition, mediators have to make sure they understand the thinking skills they and the mediatees should use in order to achieve their *mediation* goals.

(3)  *What is the content of the mediated interaction?*

The effectiveness of any mediated processes can be only achieved when they are conducted in concrete contexts the mediatees can use as a basis for learning and transcendence. As for the nature of the *mediation*, mediatees are encouraged to take an active role throughout the process, ask questions and develop a deep understanding of the subject. Consequently, mediators must base all mediated interactions on a clear context that they have studied before and whose core principles and concepts they recognise. Nevertheless, they should always look for subjects that are meaningful to the mediatees.

To conclude this phase, mediators need to collect data about mediatees' age, gender, culture, language and use of cognitive functions, thereby acknowledging previous knowledge and experiences both mediatees and mediators have of the content of the planned mediated interaction.

All the data collected about the mediatees, the mediators and the content, should be integrated through the next stage, in order to efficiently defining the goals of the mediated interaction.

*Setting goals for the mediated interaction:* Mediators wishing to mediate for better thinking development need to keep in mind two major goals: developing independent thinkers and increasing mediatees' motivation for independent learning. As mentioned previously in Chapter 2, many researchers and theoreticians agree that both intrinsic and extrinsic motivation are what drive learners to deal with cognitive challenges. Thus, mediators need to provide opportunities to increase mediatees' motivation alongside the feeling of satisfaction and the experience of cognitive challenges (Pink, 2009).

While considering ways to promote thinking development, attainment of overall goals involves focussing on more specific goals, such as which cognitive functions need to be more motivated, or which level of thinking will be challenging enough without confusing the learners. The process of considering the goals must first be based on choosing and integrating relevant criteria of *mediation* according to the parameters Feuerstein defined. Those criteria should be the basic three universal parameters (intentionality and reciprocity, transcendence and meaning), and any other relevant parameters out of the nine situational parameters reinforcing and elaborating MLE. Out of the 27 cognitive functions Feuerstein defined, it is important to choose a few from each stage of thinking – input, elaboration and output – and the level of thinking, which I recommend basing on Bloom's taxonomy of thinking skills.

In other words, the goals of mediated interaction should be defined according to four criteria: (a) which of the 12 Feuerstein's *mediation* criteria are to be used, (b) which level of thinking, (Bloom's taxonomy) will be focussed on, (c) which of the 27 cognitive functions Feuerstein defined need to be enhanced, and, (d) what stimuli for motivation will be part of the process.

While collecting all the above mentioned data was an essential process for efficient definition of the *mediation* goals, this was all necessary in order to better plan the *mediation* process.

*Scheme of Planning Mediated Interaction:* Any type of educational process should be planned according to clear parameters, but should also allow proper flexibility to change or adapt the process when needed. The planning scheme I offer here is based on clear parameters that may serve as a basis for any mediated interaction, as long as the mediators do not change the core goal of developing better thinking skills among mediatees. Nevertheless, planning according to this scheme can be done only after collection of relevant data and clear goal definition. The next two sub-chapters provide examples of how to use this planning scheme for family situations or in school.

Following the above, the scheme of the mediated interaction should include the following parameters:

- *Overall goals of the mediated interaction:* Mediators have to define for themselves why they choose to mediate during this interaction and not only to present specific knowledge, a rule or evidence as a reality that must be accepted as is. They should have one or two general goals that will guide the entire mediated interaction for intentionality and reciprocity.

- *Specific context goals that relate to the mediated situation:*
  As explained earlier, mediated interaction is a reciprocal
  process through which mediatees practice learning with
  their mediators. Therefore, efficient *mediation* must be
  related to context mediatees can use later independently.
  To succeed in creating such an efficient process, mediators
  need to define what knowledge they would like their
  mediatees to learn and use, in order to promote better
  development of proper thinking skills.

- *Specific cognitive goals for each of the mediatees:* In
  contrast to the general goals defined for the mediated
  process and for the learning content, mediators must
  define specific goals within the cognitive functions for
  each mediatee, while referring specifically to the
  stages of input, elaboration and output. Out of the
  27 cognitive functions Feuerstein defined, mediators should
  choose those that are most relevant to each mediatee
  according to his/her characteristics and the content of
  the mediated interaction, in order to promote efficient
  thinking development. The goals should refer to only a
  few cognitive functions for each mediate, and not more
  than two from each stage of thinking. Nevertheless, the
  *mediation* process can and should be conducted in groups
  to provide opportunities for peer learning and for the
  development of social skills along with any thinking skill.

- *Parameters of mediation:* Although the entire process of
  promoting thinking development is based on *mediation*,
  it is essential to decide ahead of time which of Feuerstein's
  12 parameters of *mediation* will be at the forefront. In order
  to define any interaction as mediated, it must integrate the
  three universal parameters: intentionality and reciprocity,
  meaning and transcendence. In addition, according to the
  previous goals mediators defined, they need to choose other
  relevant parameters of *mediation* out of the nine that are left.

- *Principles and main ideas:* Conducting proper processes of transcendence requires pre-organising the core ideas into clear sentences and principles. This type of organising data is based on using a high level of cognitive skills that Bloom defined as the analysis, synthesis and evaluation stages. Mediators need to phrase those principles as part of the preparation for the mediated interaction. But, as part of the *mediation* for intentionality, they also need to mediate the reasons for phrasing those principles in order to model for the mediatees how they may do this independently in the future. Nevertheless, the structure of principles needs to be clear and simple to use. If the principles are not clear enough, I would recommend to use a format such as: 'In order to… we need to…', or, 'when … then…'.

- *Outlines of the mediated interaction along with examples of bridging and transcendence:* In addition to the three universal parameters of *mediation*, the interaction is also characterised by dynamic and changeable processes. It is thus very important to prepare in writing the outlines of the planned interaction along with some possible examples for bridging and transcending at home, school, among friends and any other relevant examples. Writing the outline will provide mediators with a source to return to if the process has been changed. It will also be useful when mediators reflect on the completed *mediation* process.

*Reflective assessment:* Assessing the mediated interaction is necessary for two main reasons: (a) to learn how well the mediatees assimilated the thinking skills and processes and (b) to collect new data for efficient planning of the next mediated interaction.

Although being a mediator is based on one's reflective skills and awareness of the need to keep learning how to improve *mediation*, following the goals of the reflective phase offers another opportunity to help mediators to improve their *mediation* skills. One can learn from the process and assess its efficacy by asking the following questions: As a mediator, what did I learn about the mediatees? What did I learn about myself as a mediator? What would I change the next time I mediate to these mediatees? What do I think was effective and useful during the mediated interaction and would therefore repeat next time?

Converting theories into practices must be based on deep understanding of both the theories and the situations through which mediators wish to implement them. While there are a variety of theories in regard to *mediation* and thinking development, alongside the numerous possibilities of practicing *mediation*, it is more complex than converting one theory into one practical situation. Moreover, the risk of missing mediatees' thinking development may be realistic when novice mediators plan their first mediated interactions. From my experiences as a mediator for the last 30 years, the strategy I found the most efficient for this process is using a model with clear criteria to plan the *mediation* process and subsequently assessing its efficacy.

Throughout this section I have presented a practical perspective to integrate the cognitive theories previously examined in detail, integrating the role of the mediators and how they should relate to the mediatees and the context of knowledge. Model 2 presents my offer to plan mediated interaction while integrating the core concepts of *mediation* and thinking development introduced earlier. While using the model for planning the mediated interactions, mediators may notice the overlapping of parameters alongside the circular process. This was intentionally integrated in the model to emphasise the on-going process of *mediation*, and that the core parameters need to be integrated in all phases of *mediation*. Mediators are welcome to adjust this model to their goals and their mediatees' cognitive needs, and to develop any mediated interaction alongside any criteria of *mediation* that will contribute to the thinking development of their mediatees (Model 2 ).

**Model 2:   Planning and Conducting Thinking Development Through *Mediation*.**

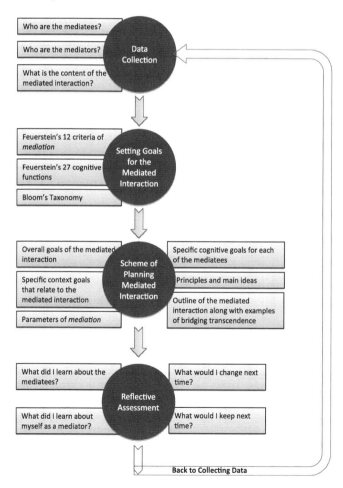

## 4.2. *MEDIATION* AND LEARNING PROCESSES IN EARLY CHILDHOOD IN A FAMILY SETTING AND ON A DAILY BASIS

Nowadays, the concept of *mediation* for thinking development and learning, usually arises while discussing school-related issues. This is despite the fact that the concept of *mediation* was developed to describe any type of interaction between people in all situations in life. Moreover, accepting *mediation* as a form of communication that everyone may use throughout life led researchers to the understanding that it should begin as early as possible in childhood, on a daily basis, not only for the sake of the young mediatees, but also in order to develop everyone's *mediation* skills (Feuerstein, 2002). From this perspective, theoreticians claiming that society is responsible for children's thinking development also emphasised the role of families in both socialisation and the thinking development among the younger generation. They based their view on the fact that families are small social units that represent their whole society, and the sooner *mediation* begins, the more efficient thinkers can develop. They also emphasised that societies must formally guide families and caregivers of young children how to become their agent of such a complex process of socialisation if they wish to develop truly independent thinkers. Moreover, formal educators should develop a dialogue with caregivers on the nature of early childhood pedagogy referring to the context of family, culture and flexible curricula (Freeman & Karlsson, 2012). From Feuerstein's perspective (Feuerstein et al., 2001), this means providing parents with valuable knowledge and skills that allow them to shift ordinary interactions into deliberately mediated ones. This perspective not only expands the family's role in their child's thinking development and learning, it actually follows Dewey's claim from 1897 (see Section 1.1) that individuals and society need to grow together through the same process and neither factor is more important than another.

Although most interactions in early childhood are almost automatic, taking on the role of mediators motivates parents and other caregivers to define goals they want to achieve as a result of their interactions: teaching basic motor skills, specific manners, vocabulary etc. Planned mediated interactions between caregivers and young mediatees promote quality achievements of the goals that will also contribute to lifelong learning. Beyond the actual learning, both the mediators and their young mediatees will experience learning as positive social interactions, while jointly conducting the learning processes is the main goal rather than the final results. Moreover, with practice, the process of planning mediated interactions becomes easier; an integral part of all daily activities. Consequently, not only will cognitive development begin early in life, but the continuum of *mediation* in schools will be only natural. Parents frequently ask at what age *mediation* may begin. Although no specific age is mentioned as a starting point for *mediation*, Feuerstein, Falik, and Feuerstein (2015) emphasise the sensitivity mediators must develop in order to understand when the child is ready to be mediated.

> *The mediational process starts very early with an important activity of the child. It starts by offering the child the option to focus visually, to create a relationship by making eye contact with the mediational figure. (p. 15)*

Although we recognise the fact that it is possible to modify our brain throughout life, psychologists and neuroscientists recommend beginning intervention in early childhood, while the brain is growing and modification is easier (Feiler & Stabio, 2018; Feuerstein et al., 2001).

Based on the *mediation* planning model presented above, below are some examples of mediated interactions than can be practiced within family situations with a focus on Feuerstein's criteria of *mediation*, thinking development and transcendence of main ideas and concepts that allows efficient practice in other situations. Mediators are welcome to adjust the examples to their goals, based on the cognitive functions of the mediatees, their previous experiences and knowledge, their age and their cultural norms. Moreover, I encourage mediators to be creative as they modify their mediated interactions.

### 4.2.1. *Mediation* in a Family Setting; Example No. 1: Family Dinner

Data Collection

*Who are the mediatees?*: Two children aged three and five. They only like to eat rice and potatoes and do not like to sit next to the table while they eat.

*Who are the mediators?*: The parents. After being at work all day, they want to have family dinners as a norm where family members communicate one with the other, along with promoting better nutrition.

*What is the content of the mediated interaction?*: Nutrition and communication.

Setting Goals for the Mediated Interaction

Feuerstein's Criteria of *Mediation*.
*Intentionality and reciprocity*: During family dinners, a variety of food is offered. Eating different types of food is important

to provide our bodies with all the necessary ingredients that promote heath and growth.

*Mediation for transcendence*: (1) Just as we need different types of food to grow healthy, we also need to have variety of colours if we wish to draw a colourful picture. (2) Communication with family during dinner creates a pleasant environment, just like communication with our friends in the playground that makes our play time much pleasanter.

*Mediation of meaning*: (1) The effect of eating different types of food follows us throughout life and therefore it is important to try new types of food and create a diverse regime of nutrition. (2) Sitting at the table during dinner allows family members to listen one to another and enjoy dinnertime beyond just the food.

*Mediation of the feeling of competence*: (1) I can take care of my health by trying new types of food. (2) I listen to the family members and contribute to the good atmosphere at the table.

*Mediation of awareness of the person as a changing entity*: Even if I did not like a certain food before, I may try it again and find out I like it.

*Mediation of the feeling of belonging*: I am part of the family and therefore I join them during dinner and contribute to the conversation.

Feuerstein's Cognitive Functions.

*Input:* clear perception along with accurate labelling of the food and the people.

*Elaboration:* selection of relevant cues in regard to the behaviour during dinner and spontaneous comparative behaviour in regard to what we eat.

*Output:* using clear and precise language while communicating.

Bloom's Taxonomy.

*Knowledge:* what are the names of the types of food? What is the proper behaviour that is expected from children during dinner?

*Comprehension:* comparing the different types of food and using proper terms for each of them.

*Application:* naming correctly all types of food, staying seated during the meal and participating in the conversation.

Given the age of the mediatees, no further thinking goals are necessary.

Scheme of Planning Mediated Interaction

*Outline of the mediated interaction that includes all the planning parameters, along with examples of bridging transcendence.*

The mediated interaction will begin as soon as the preparations for dinner begin. Parents may invite their children to set the table or prepare some of the dishes and by doing that the *mediation* for intentionality and reciprocity, alongside the *mediation* of meaning and competence begins. At that stage parents, as mediators, should verbalise the names of the foods and the desire to sit together as a family, to integrate intervention for proper use of cognitive functions and the three thinking levels of the taxonomy.

Emphasising the uniqueness of each food, during dinner parents need to name it and explain how it is different from the others (in taste, colour, texture etc.). Describing the components will provide better understanding of the differences between them and will promote communication that will lead towards achieving the goals of *mediation* for transcendence and meaning.

Mediating for competence along with *mediation* of awareness of the person as a changing entity and the feeling of belonging should continue throughout the meal, while encouraging the children to taste and name the different foods, and expressing their opinion about what they are eating. Mediators should also give positive feedback every time their children cooperate with them.

Observing mediatees' behaviour and listening to them easily allows one to observe their behaviour. The main parameter to demonstrate this process is the transcendence, which is their implementation of a new thinking process, their use of the principles in new situations. Nevertheless, the process of transcendence needs to be practiced and mediators need to model their use of it on a daily basis and not only during the mediated interaction. Therefore, throughout dinner, which was defined as the mediated interaction, parents need to emphasise the two principles: (1) from the idea that we need different types of food to grow healthy to presenting how using different ingredients allow us to develop new and creative products such as colourful pictures; (2) focussing on the importance of proper communication to create a pleasant environment in a variety of situations.

Reflective Assessment

As mentioned earlier, mediators need to assess their mediated interaction in order to learn from it for their next *mediation* interaction. The main questions that they should ask are: *What did I learn about the mediatees? What did I learn about myself as a mediator? What would I change next time? What would I keep next time?* Answering these questions can be also done by asking the mediatees directly, and then comparing their answers with the reflective perspective of the mediator.

### 4.2.3. *Mediation* in a Family Setting;
### Example No. 2: Completing a Jigsaw Puzzle

Data Collection

*Who are the mediatees?* Children who are 4-5 years old. (this mediated interaction may be conducted with one mediatee or more. But, given the age of the mediatees, I would recommend no more than three at a time.

*Who are the mediators?* A parent or caregiver, who wishes to spend quality time with the mediatee—quality time that will be beyond the fun time and include the important role of a frame or framework in life.

*What is the content of the mediated interaction?* The relations between the frame and the parts, and the role of each.

Setting Goals for the Mediated Interaction

Feuerstein's Criteria of *Mediation*.

*Intentionality and reciprocity*: While completing a jigsaw puzzle we learn how to put pieces together in order to create a given picture. To succeed, we need to collect information from the given picture and accordingly create the frame and arrange the pieces appropriately.

*Mediation of transcendence*: (1) Frames and frameworks around us serve as solid bases that hold a variety of parts. We see how window frames hold the glass, how the frame of a schedule allows us to organise what we need to do during the day, etc. (2) When we arrive somewhere new and do not know how to behave, we can look around us and learn from others, just as we learn from the picture how to build the puzzle. (3) The family is a stable framework that promotes cooperative interactions between its members.

(4) For mediatees who need higher cognitive challenges or are about to begin school: the framework of a situation, a story, or an activity may be also called the main idea that includes the core information needed for continuing with an assignment.

*Mediation of meaning*: (1) Learning from the picture how to arrange the jigsaw puzzle frame will help me complete any jigsaw puzzle on my own. (2) Learning how to build a frame helps us understand how to plan the continuum creation for anything we want to build. (3) When children behave according to the framework – the norms – it is much more pleasant to play with them.

*Mediation of the feeling of competence*: (1) I can build the jigsaw puzzle frame according to the picture on my own. (2) Using the picture as a model promotes my success in putting the jigsaw puzzle pieces together properly. (3) When I respect the rules of the family and behave accordingly, I enjoy play time much more.

*Mediation of goal seeking, goal setting and goal-achieving behaviour*: (1) Defining the goal of the play time: completing only the frame of the jigsaw puzzle; completing the whole jigsaw puzzle, etc. (2) After deciding which goal I would like to achieve, I need to plan the process towards the achievement: Where can I build the jigsaw puzzle? How many pieces do I have? How should I arrange all the pieces? What clues can I get from the picture? etc. (3) After completing the frame or the whole jigsaw puzzle, a comparison with the picture should be made in order promote behaviour comparison as well.

Feuerstein's Cognitive Functions.
*Input*: clear perception of the picture and the differentiation between the shapes of the pieces, systematic exploration for

the pieces, well-developed spatial orientation and the need for precision.

*Elaboration:* accurate definition of the problem (goal), selection of relevant cues and spontaneous comparative behaviour.

*Output:* projection of a virtual relationship, precision and accuracy and clear virtual transport.

\* The above offered cognitive functions refer mainly to the mediatees I described at the beginning of this example. Nevertheless, while mediating the same topic and ideas to older children, the *mediation* process should include more advanced cognitive functions.

Bloom's Taxonomy.

*Knowledge:* What is the goal of the jigsaw puzzle? Why are the pieces different one another? What strategy should I use?

*Comprehension:* Do I understand the meaning of the differences between the shapes? Do I understand the role of the frame?

*Application:* Putting the frame together correctly and arranging the pieces according to the picture.

*Analysis:* Categorising the pieces according to their roles and shapes; those belonging to the frame versus those belonging to the content.

*Synthesis:* Putting the pieces together.

*Evaluation:* How well and how efficiently did I complete the jigsaw puzzle?

## Scheme of Planning Mediated Interaction
*Outline of the mediated interaction that includes all the planning parameters, along with examples of bridging transcendence*

The mediated interaction will begin when the mediator suggests to the mediatees that they play together to complete a jigsaw puzzle. Parents can allow their children to choose which jigsaw puzzle they want according to the picture and the number of pieces, and decide with them where they are going to work on it. Parent may also explain why they need to prepare a flat and stable area, and how they can know how much space they will need.

Explaining the goals of the jigsaw puzzle alongside emphasising the process will prepare the mediatees for the *mediation* of transcendence that will follow. Explaining the important role of the frame can be developed from the explanation of the need to prepare the space, which is the broad frame of the interaction. The *mediation* of transcendence may be continued while categorising the pieces into two groups according to their role as part of the frame or the middle content, just as the parent and the child are completing the jigsaw puzzle together, but each has a different role in the process.

Promoting the development of the cognitive functions mentioned above should be by focussing on the processes along with explaining their meaning. Success in completing a jigsaw puzzle is based on well-developed spatial orientation. But, this can be achieved only when the mediatees learn how to select relevant cues and compare them with the picture as the model. Mediatees also need to be precise and develop clear virtual transport, such as they do when they draw a picture they have seen before, or when they try imitate someone else's behaviour.

One of the main challenges young children face when completing a jigsaw puzzle is the frustration of not finding a specific piece they are looking for. It is, thus, essential to promote the development of the cognitive function from the output phase; the systematic exploration and to explain to the mediatees the importance of this function in other areas in life such as looking for a specific toy, playing hide and seek etc.

The main principles leading this mediated interaction refer to the role of frames and the interaction with the parts: (1) Putting the frame together correctly promotes efficient completion of the jigsaw puzzle, just as behaving according to norms allows us to enjoy a game much more. (2) Categorising the pieces according their role in the jigsaw puzzle helps complete it efficiently; just as putting our things where they belong makes it easier to find them when needed.

### Reflective Assessment

As mentioned earlier, mediators need to assess their mediated interaction in order to learn from it for their next *mediation* interaction. The main questions that they should ask are: *What did I learn about the mediatees? What did I learn about myself as a mediator? What would I change next time? What would I keep next time?* Answering these questions can be also done by asking the mediatees directly, and then comparing their answers with the reflective perspective of the mediator.

## 4.2.4. *Mediation* in a Family Setting; Example No. 3: 'Arguing versus Discussing'

Conducting conversations and efficient discussions where different points of view are welcome without causing any arguments is a complex communication skill that is usually not worked on at an early age. Nevertheless, this skill can be mediated within families and may promote enjoyable times together.

Data Collection

*Who are the mediatees?* Siblings aged 8–12.

*Who are the mediators?* Parents.

*What is the content of the mediated interaction?* In many cases, siblings tend to rush into arguments instead of discussing their different points of view. Although the content of these arguments may not be of significance, their impact is. These arguments damage family encounters and may drive both parents and siblings to avoid further interactions. While considering the content of this mediated interaction, mediators should bear in mind that the mediatees are on the verge of adolescence; a period characterised by their search of identity by breaching borders. Therefore, *mediation* towards family conversations should also motivate each of the mediatees to express their needs and thoughts.

## Setting Goals for the Mediated Interaction

Feuerstein's Criteria of *Mediation*.

*Intentionality and reciprocity*: Spending time with family is the basis for developing social interaction alongside the fun all the family can experience. Nevertheless, not all members think the same or agree upon everything, and so we need to learn to accept others' points of view and find the middle ground for good relations.

*Mediation for transcendence*: While taking part in social activities in all areas in life we will meet different people who think differently than us. Nevertheless, if we want to be part of these activities, we need to understand their perceptions, to present ours, and find the way to live together.

*Mediation of meaning*: If I wish to spend time with the family in order to play or do something else with them, not all of them will agree. I don't need to get upset and argue with them, I need to listen to their answers, to present my point of

view and then discuss with them what will be the most efficient solution for everyone.

*Mediation of sharing behaviour*: When people do not
understand what I want and therefore upset me, I need to
share with them how I feel and why would I like to do certain
things. Other people cannot read my thoughts even if they are
part of my family and they have known me for many years.

*Mediation of individuation and psychological differentia-
tion*: Different people may think differently and therefore it is
acceptable for me to think and feel differently as well.

*Mediation of awareness of the person as a changing entity*:
Listening to others allows me learning different perspectives.
Consequently, it is natural to change my perspective and agree
with people I did not agree with before. The same process
of changing may occur with others, where they change their
perspectives after I present my opinions clearly and logically.

*Mediation of the feeling of belonging*: No matter if I think
differently than the rest of the family; I still belong to the family and can find the way to join in family meetings.

Feuerstein's Cognitive Functions.
*Input*: clear perception of the situation, need for precision,
accuracy and completeness in data gathering, capacity to consider more than one source of information.

*Elaboration*: Accurate definition of the problem, using logical evidence to arrive at and defend a conclusion, internalisation of information and inferential hypothetical thinking.

*Output*: Using clear and precise language, communicating
the answer and waiting before responding.

Bloom's Taxonomy.
*Knowledge*: What do I know about the situation? What do I
know about others' perspectives?

*Comprehension*: Do I understand why other people think
differently than me? Do I understand their point of view?

*Application*: Presenting my point of view clearly while respecting other perspectives.

*Analysis*: Organising my goals while comparing them to the goals of other family members'

*Synthesis*: Finding the core link between all the family members' goals.

*Evaluation*: Did the family enjoy our time together? What factors contributed to success or caused failure?

Scheme of Planning Mediated Interaction
*Outline of the mediated interaction that includes all the planning parameters, along with examples of bridging transcendence*

Family activities are conducted on a daily basis and most of them even as a routine without any special preparations. Conversations, as well, take place as a simple skill people employ, and usually there is no special preparation to conduct conversations within the family. As a result, when siblings do not agree on something, if they do not recognise the communication skills they need to convince others of their idea, or do not understand why they should listen to others, arguments begin to develop. Therefore, parents first need to mediate towards ways of discussion on the basis of relatively simple topics such as what to prepare for dinner, what game to play after dinner, what family activity to plan for the weekend, how to assign house-chores among everyone, etc. This example will focus on discussion about which music to listen to while driving on the way to a picnic with friends at the weekend.

The mediated interaction will begin before leaving the house, in order to allow relaxed conversation and later to enjoy the day. This can also be done a day or more beforehand. Parents may share with their children the plans for a picnic day with their friends and emphasise how everyone is going to enjoy the day. This will also be a good opportunity to mediate for individuation (each one will play with his/her friends) alongside *mediation* of the feeling of belonging (we are all together). Increasing their motivation to meet their friends will ease the discussion about the issue that causes arguments; the music they will listen on the way. After everyone knows which of their friends is coming, parents need to say where the picnic will take place and how long it may take to get there. Then, the can bring up the question: what music would you like to listen to on the way?

At this point, *mediation* is crucial. Since the parents' main goal is develop conversation skills, they should ask each of the siblings to explain why they would like this specific music. Nevertheless, parents should also say what music they want to listen to and explain their choice. This mediated process contributes to the *mediation* of meaning alongside the *mediation* of intentionality, whereas the *mediation* of transcendence can be emphasised by asking the children to think of situations in which they have an option to choose and then to explain how they make their choices.

Understanding the reasons for choosing different types of music must be presented by participants with appropriate cognitive empathy. This can be reached when each one expresses at least one positive criterion for all the choices. Then, the total time of driving may be equally divided among all the types of songs that were chosen. If the process is conducted ahead of time, the siblings may prepare a playlist of all the songs, including those the parents like. It is important that no one give up the option to choose his/her favourite music, in order to promote *mediation* for the feeling of belonging, along with emphasising that different people with different choices can find a way to spend enjoyable time together.

One option that may be offered by the children is that each one can listen to his/her favourite music with headphones. Children may also explain that by doing so they will not argue and they will keep the atmosphere relaxed on a long drive together. On one hand, this offer may be efficient once in a while, when each one wishes to have quiet time on his/her own. But, by allowing this type of solution we actually prevent the *mediation* of the main principle: expressing my opinions together with understanding the reasons for people having other opinions promotes experiencing a diverse society in which different people enjoy living together.

Reflective Assessment

As mentioned earlier, mediators need to assess their mediated interaction in order to learn from it for their next *mediation* interaction. The main questions that they should ask are: *What did I learn about the mediatees? What did I learn about myself as a mediator? What would I change next time? What would I keep next time?* Answering these questions can be also done by asking the mediatees directly, and then comparing their answers with the reflective perspective of the mediator.

## 4.2.5. *Mediation* in a Family Setting; Example No. 4: Getting Ready for School

Getting to school on time is a rule all students are aware of. Students also know that not following this rule may cause them to suffer consequences. Nevertheless, many parents report that getting their children to school on time challenges them almost on a daily basis. From another perspective, in many cases, taking the children to school late causes parents to get to work late as well. Moreover, the stress children and their parents experience in the morning affects them throughout the rest of the day. The mediated interaction presented here offers an opportunity to mediate the meaning of scheduling, the importance of keeping to a schedule and how not keeping to it can affect the parents' schedule.

Researchers who studied and developed several theories of cognitive and thinking development stress that the awareness of time and the organisation skill of 'being on time' is a cultural factor that can significantly influence cognitive development in this area. For example, in some cultures, arrive on time for a dinner invitation will be what is expected, whereas in others you may be expected to arrive a few minutes earlier or later. Thus, while preparing a mediated interaction based on proper uses of temporal concepts and orientation in time, mediators should recognise the mediatees' culture of origin in addition to the culture they are living in.

## Data Collection

*Who are the mediatees?* Children who attend elementary school and are dependent on their parents' help to get to school.

*Who are the mediators?* Parents.

*What is the content of the mediated interaction?* The importance of getting ready for school on time in order to have a relaxing and enjoyable day.

## Setting Goals for the Mediated Interaction:

Feuerstein's Criteria of *Mediation*.

*Intentionality and reciprocity*: Succeeding in getting to school on time is based on efficient planning and cooperation between parents and children. It also affects the feeling of the family members through the rest of the day.

*Mediation for transcendence*: Planning and arriving on time is essential in a variety of activities and we may miss important things when we are late. For example, if we arrive late for a movie we will miss the beginning or we might even miss the whole movie because we will not be allowed in late so we don't disturb those who came on time; if we get to the playground late we may find out that our friends have begun to play a team game without us and don't want to start all over again; if we are late to the train station, the train will go without us and we will have to wait for the next one.

*Mediation of meaning*: (1) Planning my schedule ahead of time allows me to have a relaxing morning (2) Getting to school on time contributes to my teachers' appreciation of me. (3) When I realise that I cannot organise my time in the morning, I can always ask my parents for help because this is the goal for all of us.

*Mediation of competence*: (1) I can plan my steps ahead of time and get to school on time. (2) I can contribute to my parents' efficiency at work by cooperating with them while getting ready in the morning.

*Mediation of feeling of belonging*: Everyone in the family has roles in the morning and only if we are all responsible to fulfil them will we all get wherever we are going on time.

Feuerstein's Cognitive Functions.

*Input*: clear perception of the tasks that need to be completed, well-developed orientation in space and time, capacity to consider more than one source of information at once.

*Elaboration*: accurate definition of the problem, selection of relevant cues about the time and the tasks that need to be completed, integrating a variety of data from different sources, planning behaviour.

*Output*: projecting of virtual relationships of time and space while organising precision and accuracy, clear visual transport.

Bloom's Taxonomy.

*Knowledge:* What tasks need to be completed and who is responsible for each one, at what time do I need to be ready?

*Comprehension:* Estimating the time I need to complete my tasks, understanding the effects of not completing them on time.

*Application:* Demonstrating an efficient and organised process of completing the tasks and getting to school on time.

*Analysis:* Breaking down my tasks into smaller ones.

*Synthesis:* Completing all the tasks in logical order.

*Evaluation:* Comparing my actual organisation to what was planned originally and evaluating what could be done better next time (even if I got to school on time, I can always be more efficient).

## Scheme of Planning Mediated Interaction

*Outline of the mediated interaction that includes all the planning parameters, along with examples of bridging transcendence*

Getting to school on time is the end of a complex process based mainly on the understanding of time, schedule and organisation. In addition, this process is also influenced by the motivation one has to get to school on time; motivation that may develop from both extrinsic and intrinsic factors.

Therefore, parents and caregivers should make mediatees be aware of the concepts of time and schedule on a daily basis. The main temporal concepts needed for this mediated interaction are: early, late, on time, later, before. Because the temporal concepts are abstract and the *mediation* is with elementary school students, in addition to the proper use of the concepts, *mediation* of the practical meaning of time should also include an example of the 'amount' of time. Mediators may express it by integrating the concepts more clearly as they describe processes and procedures. For example, they may say: 'It will take water 10 minutes to boil and then we can add the pasta to the cooking pot', or,

> *Because we need to leave the house in an hour, and*
> *it takes an hour and a half for the washing machine*
> *to finish a cycle, we will start it only when we*
> *return.*

As mentioned above, this mediated interaction is based on the assumption that mediatees recognise the basic temporal concepts, and that they have previous knowledge about their meanings and proper uses. Nevertheless, throughout the interaction mediators should make sure that concepts are clear for all mediatees.

Planning the morning schedule should begin at least the day before, because we want to include mediated interaction through the process of planning, and to promote mediatees' motivation towards reciprocity. The mediated interaction should begin with parents' intentionality, as they present their goals and explanations for the need to get to school on time. Beyond the obvious expectation to get to school on time, pre-organising the morning schedule and succeeding in executing the plan allows parents also to get to work on time in a more relaxed mood that will influence the rest of the day. From that, the *mediation* of meaning for the mediatees is also that by cooperating with their parents during morning activities and being ready for school on time, they help their parents have a better day. Moreover, the mediatees themselves will have a pleasant day because they will not be stressed in the morning and no one will be upset with them when they get to school.

Regarding the age of the children, planning the morning schedule should be concrete and visual. I suggest preparing with the children a chart in which all the essential morning activities are written with the name of the family member responsible for them. For example, next to 'dressing' all members' names will be written, but next to 'preparing sandwiches' everyday a different person will be responsible. This type of chart can also be used to mediate for the feeling of belonging, because each one contributes to the success of the goal of getting to school on time.

Reflective Assessment

As mentioned earlier, mediators need to assess their mediated interaction in order to learn from it for their next *mediation* interaction. The main questions that they should ask are: *What did I learn about the mediatees? What did I learn about myself as a mediator? What would I change next time? What would I keep next time?* Answering these questions can be also done by asking the mediatees directly, and then comparing their answers with the reflective perspective of the mediator.

## 4.3. *MEDIATION* AND LEARNING PROCESSES IN THE CLASSROOM

Throughout this book, *mediation* is presented as a basic process that should be integrated in all areas of life, from birth onwards. Nevertheless, given the structured nature of classroom learning, society has developed a perspective according to which there is a direct and logical connection between thinking development and learning in schools. As a result, society regards educators as those who are exclusively responsible for the development of thinking processes. On the basis of different theories and studies, I previously suggested that parents should begin promoting thinking development in early childhood using a *mediation* approach, but this does not reduce in any way the responsibility of educators to continue the process in school. Integrating thinking development perspectives alongside pedagogy and teaching approaches leads towards the essential need to develop curricula which present the relations between acquiring knowledge and developing appropriate thinking skills (Haywood, 2004).

The main theories and concepts of learning, thinking development, and *mediation* serve as an important basis for educators to plan and conduct mediated interactions for thinking development, as will be presented in this part of the book. Beyond the success of developing thinking development, practicing *mediation* while teaching subject matter is the most efficient way to develop independent learners who understand how they can learn new material on their own and become self-mediators when dealing with new challenges. Mediators from all areas of education must believe in their ability to conduct such thinking development processes, but, they should do it only on the basis of integrating *mediation* perspectives along with pedagogical, psychological and neuropedagogical aspects; choosing only one perspective will not allow an efficient mediated process. Moreover, educators need to keep learning from new neuropedagogy studies and integrate it within all disciplines in order to better modify learners' brain and thinking development (Friedman et al., 2019). Nevertheless, success of this integrated learning process is also based on mediators' professional knowledge of the subject they teach. Following are a few mediated teaching-learning sessions that can be implemented within the core domains taught in most schools: reading, writing, science and mathematics.

Whereas the family context focussed on possible mediated interactions conducted among family and friends, with only a few mediatees at a time, the school context presents the process of *mediation* through teaching in large groups and therefore planning is even more essential. To allow mediators an opportunity to better understand how to implement the proposed *mediation* model, the mediated sessions presented here focus on daily learning situations in elementary schools, according to age, cognitive skills and discipline. It is, of course, up to the mediators to adjust the process according to the culture and characteristics of their students alongside the knowledge they would like to mediate their mediatees.

### 4.3.1. *Mediation* in the Classroom; Example No.1: Why Should We Come to School?

Moving from kindergarten to 1st grade in school is a complex process that needs to be carefully mediated in order to increase children's intrinsic motivation to deal with the new challenges they may face. Beyond the new and cognitive challenging situations children face in school, transitioning from a relative warm, caring, child-centred kindergarten environment to a potentially less flexible environment, the 1st-grade classroom is also a struggle for many children and their caregivers (Sink, Edwards, & Weir, 2007). However, many educators and caregivers miss this opportunity to mediate for cognitive development while providing cognitive skills for better adjustment, because they address the process as a simple transfer from one learning environment to another that everyone undergoes.

Although the following mediated example focusses on interaction between mediators and 1st-graders, the need to promote intrinsic motivation among students may be relevant for all students in all grades and mediators are encourage to modify the example as needed.

Data Collection

*Who are the mediatees?* 1ˢᵗ-grade students.

*Who are the mediators?* The home room teacher.

*What is the content of the mediated interaction?* Increasing motivation to come and study in the school environment.

## Setting Goals for the Mediated Interaction

Feuerstein's Criteria of *Mediation.*

*Intentionality and reciprocity*: (1) Schools were developed in order to allow all children learn a variety of subjects together with new friends. (2) Teachers are trained to teach all children all the necessary knowledge that will allow them in the future to become independent learners. (3) Students come to school to acquire new knowledge, develop new learning skills and meet new friends.

*Mediation of transcendence*: (1) Participating in new environments such as schools is like learning new games. (2) Learning from my teachers in order to become an independent learner is like learning from my parents to do things on my own (getting dressed, eating, taking a shower, etc.)

*Mediation of meaning*: (1) Becoming an independent learner will allow me to become independent in other things as well. (2) Meeting new friend will open up new opportunities for me for afternoon activities.

*Mediation of the feeling of competence*: (1) Coming to school is the proof that I am mature enough to learn new challenging things. (2) I can learn with new friends. (3) I can become an independent learner if I follow the learning processes in school. (4) I can study all day long in school although the activities are not the same as in kindergarten.

*Mediation of the awareness of the person as a changing entity*: As a school student I can change my habits of playing and begin learning complicated topics alongside adjusting to school's schedule and demands.

*Mediation of the feeling of belonging*: (1) When I come to school I learn and play with new friends and teachers. (2) In school I can help my new friends adjust to school by sharing my thought and feelings with them.

Feuerstein's Cognitive Functions.

*Input:* Clear perception of the new structure of school and the daily schedule, precise and accurate labelling of the subject matters studied, well-developed orientation in space, in time, capacity to consider more than one source of information.

*Elaboration:* Spontaneous comparative behaviour to shift from kindergarten to the school environment and to allow focussing on the advantages of school, broad mental fields and memory, integrating a variety of data from different domains and learning situations, planning behaviour and use of adequate verbal tools and elaboration of certain cognitive categorisations.

*Output:* Using clear and precise language, communicating answers, using adequate verbal tools and clear visual transport.

Bloom's Taxonomy.

*Knowledge:* What subjects do I study in school? Where is my classroom? What do I need to bring with me to school?

*Comprehension:* Do I understand what I am expected to do in school? Do I understand my role in school? Do I understand how to use the things I bring from home efficiently when I am at school?

*Application:* How do I learn and behave in school? What learning skills do I use?

*Analysis:* What specific subjects do I learn at school? Who are my new friends in school?

*Synthesis:* What learning activities can I do with my friends?

*Evaluation*: What things can I learn and do at school that I could not in kindergarten?

## Scheme of Planning Mediated Interaction
*(Outline of the mediated interaction that includes all the planning parameters, along with examples of bridging transcendence)*

Promoting children's motivation to leave behind the kindergarten environment; flexible activities, play time and a lot of attention from the teachers, is a process that must be cognitively mediated towards the advantages of academic learning alongside the *mediation* of the feeling of competence and of the awareness of the person as a changing entity. This should be achieved, without causing the students any uncomfortable feelings if they miss kindergarten once in a while. Therefore, *mediation* by the homeroom teacher should begin from the first day of school.

Knowing your students is the most important factor that contributes to the success of any *mediation* process you want to prepare. Therefore, before planning how to increase their motivation to succeed in meeting the new challenges school offers, mediators must learn about mediatees' feelings and experiences in kindergarten. I suggest that all teachers and mediators dedicate the first few days of school to get to know their new students better. Whereas there are varieties of ways mediators can learn about their mediatees, following the theories presented earlier in first chapter of this book, mediators should allow mediatees to introduce themselves from their perspective of their strengths. As Gardner (2011) claimed, people may learn and present their knowledge by using one of the seven intelligences. Accordingly, I suggest that homeroom teachers, as mediators, prepare different activities that will encourage the new students to express themselves comfortably.

One important factor that school teachers and mediators should remember is that, in kindergarten, children are encouraged to develop their creativity and to express themselves using original means. Hence, just before they learn that in school they are expected to present their knowledge according to specific criteria, allowing them to choose their own way will strength their self-confidence in the new environment alongside the opportunity for the mediators to learn about the mediatees' strengths.

One important factor that school teachers and mediators should remember is that, in kindergarten, children are encouraged to develop their creativity and to express themselves using original means. Hence, just before they learn that in school they are expected to present their knowledge according to specific criteria, allowing them to choose their own way will strength their self-confidence in the new environment alongside the opportunity for the mediators to learn about the mediatees' strengths.

Following mediatees' answers, mediators better recognise the strengths of their mediatees and their topics of interest. To increase mediatees' feeling of competence alongside the feeling of belonging, mediators may plan now other activities into which they have integrated the new information. This way, mediatees will understand that their voice is heard and considered. Moreover, if the homeroom teachers, the mediators, integrate some of the mediatees' favourite activities from kindergarten, they will mediate for the awareness of the person as a changing entity, as they show that the same activities can be conducted in different environments.

After a few days in school, when mediators develop better understanding of who their mediatees are, more challenging assignments may be integrated to increase mediatees' feeling of belonging. These assignments should focus on the mediatees' answers to the third question alongside assignments that promote better recognition of the school environment, such as how to get to the office, what are the different routes to the playground etc. The third phase of activities can already integrate assignments that focus on solving basic problems while cooperating with peers. For example: what may I do if I forget my pencil case? Who can I approach if I miss home during the day? What can I do if I see one of my classmates is unhappy?

Given that all the above activities are developed in the school environment in order to develop mediatees' motivation to come to school, mediators have to conclude each one with a summary of what each one has learned and how they are going to use this knowledge in school and elsewhere. This type of summary will emphasise the role of school as a place to study things that will contribute to us elsewhere.

### Reflective Assessment

As mentioned earlier, mediators need to assess their mediated interaction in order to learn from it for their next *mediation* interaction. The main questions that they should ask are: *What did I learn about the mediatees? What did I learn about myself as a mediator? What would I change next time? What would I keep next time?* Answering these questions can be also done by asking the mediatees directly, and then comparing their answers with the reflective perspective of the mediator.

### 4.3.2. *Mediation* in the Classroom; Example No. 2: Learning to Write

Reading and writing are basic skills that are used to study any other domain, and educators refer to them as the keys to success in school and in life (Cohen, Mather, Schneider, & White, 2017). Hence they are taught from first day of school, and children are expected to develop their reading and writing skills with minimum effort. This is, without referring to the fact that teaching reading and writing requires explicit pedagogical training that must be adjusted to the children's culture, language or special needs (Langeberg, 2019). Both reading and writing are complex skills that involve a variety of cognitive operations and a high level of thinking skills, alongside language skills and cultural awareness (Biria & Liaghat, 2018). Nevertheless, teaching writing should begin only after children have succeeded in learning basic reading skills.

Writing is a skill one uses in order to express feelings, thoughts, opinions, etc. Although there are several levels of writing and self-expression, the process basically requires cognitive development to deal simultaneously with several interwoven micro-skills such as developing an idea, capturing the mental effort of thinking out sentences, translating sentences into proper language in a meaningful communicative manner (Biria & Liaghat, 2018). Following these preparations, to perform the actual writing – to translate the cognitive processes into visual language – one needs to coordinate between the cognitive processes and fine motor skills. Nevertheless, expressing oneself in writing should be in a language that other people will be eager to read and understand what one wanted to communicate.

In addition to the fact that writing is already a complex process, teaching writing and *mediating* the importance of writing should be carefully handled in order to increase mediatees intrinsic motivation while encouraging creativity in writing, even though mediators, friends or strangers may give feedback and sometimes even criticise the final product (Langeberg, 2019).

## Data Collection

*Who are the mediatees?* 1st and 2nd grade students who already acquired the basic reading skills.

*Who are the mediators?* The homeroom teacher.

*What is the content of the mediated interaction?* Motivating students to improve their writing skills and their ability to express themselves in writing.

## Setting Goals for the Mediated Interaction

Feuerstein's Criteria of *Mediation.*

*Intentionality and reciprocity*: (1) Writing is a skill that allows self-expression via a different medium. (2) Writing is one of the main forms of communication people use around the world.

*Mediation for transcendence*: Although writing is a skill we study in school, it is mostly used in other situations such as writing notes for my parents at home, text messaging to my friends, etc.

*Mediation of meaning*: (1) Learning how to write will allow me to better express my knowledge in a range of subject matters. (2) Writing on my own will allow me to communicate with my family and friends independently.

*Mediation of feeling of competence*: (1) I can write my answers clearly (2) I can express my thoughts in writing (3) I can communicate in writing like my parents and friends do.

*Mediation of regulation and control of behaviour*: (1) In order to be able to write clearly, I need to control my fine motor behaviour and project words into visual form. (2) When I write, I choose what to share with others by controlling the process of expression.

*Mediation of individuation and psychological differentiation*: writing allows me to be active and present what I think and feel, whereas in reading I and more passive and I read only what other people have decided to share with me.

*Mediation of the feeling of belonging*: Writing is one of the communication skills people use in my environment and by being able to write I can better integrate into the society around me.

Feuerstein's Cognitive Functions.
*Input:* Clear perception of the shape and sound of the letters, precise and accurate labelling, well-developed spatial orientation in order to write the letters correctly and organise the writing on the page, well-developed time orientation in order to develop efficient writing processes and the capacity to consider more than one source of information to allow proper use of spelling.

*Elaboration:* Selection of relevant cues of letters and sounds, integrating a variety of data such as the correct spelling of a word, using logical evidence, planning behaviour in regard to the way to write and the space I should use for writing.

*Output:* Using clear and precise language, projection of virtual relationships, communication the answer, clear visual transport.

Bloom's Taxonomy.
*Knowledge:* recognising all the letters and how we pronounce each one as a separate letter or when letters appear with others. For example, the sound of the letter *s* versus the sound of the letters *sh*.

*Comprehension:* Understanding how to use the letters when I wish to integrate them into a word.

*Application:* Writing words and sentences using correct spelling.

*Analysis:* What letters do I need to create a certain word? What words do I need to express myself correctly through a structured sentence?

*Synthesis:* Using proper letters and words to express myself in writing.

*Evaluation:* Did I use the right spelling and concepts to express myself in writing?

Scheme of Planning Mediated Interaction

*Outline of the mediated interaction that includes all the planning parameters, along with examples of bridging transcendence*

As mentioned above, writing is an academic skill studied in school in order to allow students to express feelings, thoughts, opinions, etc. Nevertheless, writing is a complex skill that challenges learners mainly since they have not all acquired the fine motor skills yet, and our role is to make sure all learners succeed in writing. Keeping writing as a challenging process and not a frustrating one demands the use of *mediation* to teach such a basic academic skill, promote thinking development among students as they realise that they may express what they wish independently and may also control what others know about them. The wish to be independent and to control what and how you express yourself is the core motivating factor to deal with the challenge of writing. Therefore, this is the path along which homeroom teachers – the mediators – should base their *mediation*.

Learning how to write usually proceeds on the assumption that mediatees have already learned basic reading skills and that they are acquainted with the role of written language since caregivers read them stories before and since customarily they are introduced to reading before writing. Moreover, recognising a written letter, labelling it and knowing which sound or sounds can be produced with it is the basis for both reading and writing. Therefore, *mediation* of the feeling of competence – I already know how to read the letters – is essential for dealing with the challenge of writing.

As mentioned above, the main goals or intentions of the process are to allow mediatees to express themselves through a different medium, and to allow them to develop new opportunities to communicate with people. Therefore, these intentions should be clearly integrated into all mediated activities so that the mediatees are aware of them. Although in school different subjects are often taught by different teachers, in 1st and 2nd grade the homeroom teachers usually teach most of them, and therefore it will ease the *mediation* process for writing. It is important that mediators mediate writing as a skill that promotes learning in all other domains. This way, the *mediation* of transcendence is easier and mediatees can implement the writing skill independently.

For example, given the age of the mediatees, it is important to begin each school day with a review of the learning activities planned for that day. While doing so, each mediatee should use an individual graphic table in which he/she writes the subjects and the specific content or assignments on their own. Mediatees do not need to be expert writers for this activity, because they can copy the information from the board; an essential visual and cognitive skill they should practice for better cognitive development. The advantages of this morning preparation are mainly: mediatees will be mediated towards individuation because they will have their own chart on which they can evaluate what they studied or not at the end of the day, mediatees' orientation in space and time will be improved because they practice writing in a table and better understand the schedule of the day, mediatees may also ask questions in regard to the schedule and share their thoughts with others, and they will be able to use the idea of planning other activities in a chart as well.

Another example of using writing as an integrated skill is a mediated interaction towards the end of the school day. Once again, given the age of the mediatees, the school day may be overwhelming and they may need some *mediation* to help them summarise the core of each learning day. Towards the end of each day, the homeroom teacher should review with the mediatees what were they did during the day, leading the discussion by using terms that describe what were they learning at school. An example of learning can be taken from any subject matter or play time with class peers, the focus should be on 'what have you learned today' or 'in what did you succeed today?' Such questions mainly increase the feeling of competence along with the feeling of individuation and the human as a changing entity. During conversation, homeroom teachers may write all the examples on the board to promote sharing behaviour and the feeling of belonging, along with practicing reading. At this stage, after all mediatees express verbally what they learned or what they succeeded in doing, each one will write in his/her notebook the sentence that presents their best summary of the day. Mediatees may copy from the board what they teacher wrote while they spoke, or, they may also write something new. When learners have an individual notebook that contains what they studied, they can always go back and read what they have written to refresh their memory along with promoting their feeling of competence as writers.

Both examples of the above examples emphasise the active role mediatees have while writing, their opportunities to express themselves, and the advantage of using written information.

### Reflective Assessment

As mentioned earlier, mediators need to assess their mediated interaction in order to learn from it for their next *mediation* interaction. The main questions that they should ask are: *What did I learn about the mediatees? What did I learn about myself as a mediator? What would I change next time? What would I keep next time?* Answering these questions can be also done by asking the mediatees directly, and then comparing their answers with the reflective perspective of the mediator.

### 4.3.3. *Mediation* in the Classroom;
### Example No. 3: The Four Arithmetic Operations

Mathematics is taught in the majority of countries as a mandatory subject for all students. Whereas the overall reason and goal for teaching math is to promote proper use of concepts in order to investigate, learn about and solve problems on a daily basis, teachers focus on concrete knowledge and basic math problems with no further implementation (Gningue, Peach, & Schroder, 2013). As a result, while assessing students' understanding as they study new topics in math, their achievements are much lower than expected and researchers claim than students do not understand the meaning of mathematical procedures and the possibilities of using math knowledge outside the classroom (Bender & Crane, 2011). Although the reasons for these difficulties can be examined from different perspectives, viewing thinking development as the main goal of education, leads to two main explanations alongside possibilities for changes: (a) from Bloom's perspective of the taxonomy of thinking, basing mathematics learning mainly on the acquisition of new knowledge prevents students from using it when they need to understand or implement it at higher levels of thinking. (b) From Feuerstein's MLE approach, the lack of *mediation* of meaning and transcendence prevents students from using their basic knowledge in other learning opportunities.

Asking how mathematical thinking develops and what factors may contribute to the efficiency of this development led variety of researchers recognising the contribution of well-developed orientation in space to the development of efficient mathematical thinking (Mix & Cheng, 2012; Nilges & Usnick, 2000). Therefore, mediating for thinking development on the basis of teaching mathematics must be alongside mediating for better spatial orientation.

## Data Collection

*Who are the mediatees?* 2nd- and 3rd-grade students.

*Who are the mediators?* The math teacher.

*What is the content of the mediated interaction?* How to solve math exercises involving the use of the four basic arithmetic operations.

## Setting Goals for the Mediated Interaction

Feuerstein's Criteria of *Mediation*.

*Intentionality and reciprocity*: Understanding the role of each arithmetic operation and the relations between them will allow efficient coping with math assignments.

*Mediation of transcendence*: Complex assignments can be dealt with efficiently when analysing and categorising the data according to the characteristics of each parameter. For example, when I need to prepare my school bag, I can check what subjects I will study the following day according to the weekly schedule, and then I will check what materials I need for each class. Only then I will organise everything in the school bag.

*Mediation of meaning*: Being able to solve a math exercise that includes all four arithmetic operations will allow me to solve other complex assignments as well.

*Mediation of competence*: I can cope with complex assignments by analysing them into the role of each element.

*Mediation of awareness of the person as a changing entity*: Using correct strategies and following instructions allow me to become a better math student and solve math problems I could not before.

Feuerstein's Cognitive Functions.

*Input:* Clear perception of the arithmetic concepts and operations, precise and accurate labelling, well-developed orientation in space, capacity of consider more than one source of information.

*Elaboration:* Accurate definition of the problem, selection of relevant cues, using logical evidence to arrive at and defend a conclusion.

*Output:* Projection of virtual relationships, using adequate verbal tools, waiting before responding.

Bloom's Taxonomy.

*Knowledge:* What is the role of each one of the arithmetic operations?

*Comprehension:* How do arithmetic operations contribute to the process of solving the math exercise?

*Application:* Using the proper arithmetic operation in the proper phase to solve the math exercise.

*Analysis:* Recognising and categorising the arithmetic operations according to their role and the process of solving the exercise.

*Synthesis:* Organising the process of solving the math exercise by logically integrating relevant arithmetic operations.

*Evaluation:* Did I use the proper strategy to solve the math exercise? Does my answer logically relate to the problem presented in the exercise? Did I conclude the exercise correctly?

## Scheme of Planning Mediated Interaction

*Outline of the mediated interaction that includes all the planning parameters, along with examples of bridging transcendence*

Dealing with math assignments is an abstract action that requires integrating a variety of cognitive skills. Although most children in 2nd and 3rd grade are able to solve math exercises for each of the basic arithmetic operations (addition, subtraction, multiplication and division), when they face an exercise that integrates more than one operation they often suddenly display frustration and confusion. The main reason for their lack of competence evolves from the fact they practiced solving exercises automatically without understanding the logic for each operation, and without developing any significant cognitive skill. Moreover, the process of learning arithmetic operations usually does not integrate any significant applications for life, and the learning process becomes relevant solely for math classes. Therefore, while planning this mediated interaction for this group of students, *mediation* for transcendence, meaning and competence is essential.

Coping with assignments that integrate different types of knowledge and cognitive skills can be done only on a basis of well-structured understanding. Therefore, the *mediation* process should begin with activities that promote organisation of previous knowledge according to clear parameters. These activities may include peer work to promote the *mediation* for competence alongside the *mediation* for sharing behaviour and belonging. Organising data in charts will promote both the orientation in space and the use of precise and accurate concepts, whereas presenting situations in life for the use of each arithmetic operation will develop better transcendence.

Only after all mediatees present proper understanding of each of the four arithmetic operations, may integrating them begin. I suggest that math teachers, as the mediators, begin the process from the *mediation* of meaning and transcendence from the mediatees' perspective. For example, ask each mediatee to write few parameters that they believe characterise them. Then, give them an assignment that they have to do in groups of four, and ask them to make sure that they integrate their characteristics throughout the process and the result. Afterwards, discuss with the mediatees the process they used to succeed, and present them the analogy to math exercises that include all four arithmetic operations.

Only at this stage, when mediatees understand the overall idea of integrating several arithmetic operations together, may mediators present the rules mediatees should follow when solving such exercises: multiplication and division should be conducted before addition and subtraction. However, learning this arithmetic principle is actually another stage for more complex arithmetic operations, and must therefore be performed alongside practice and implementation in a variety of assignments. By learning alongside practicing in other situations in life, mediatees will develop better cognitive skills that will allow them to cope with new math tasks on the basis of thinking rather than with automatic actions that may not be efficient.

The main principle that should lead mediators through this content and promote proper transcendence is: when I have an assignment that requires more than one operation, it is important to organise the process according to the role and significance of each operation. Accordingly, I should plan the strategy and complete the assignment step by step.

Reflective Assessment

As mentioned earlier, mediators need to assess their mediated interaction in order to learn from it for their next *mediation* interaction. The main questions that they should ask are: *What did I learn about the mediatees? What did I learn about myself as a mediator? What would I change next time? What would I keep next time?* Answering these questions can be also done by asking the mediatees directly, and then comparing their answers with the reflective perspective of the mediator.

### 4.3.4. *Mediation* in the Classroom; Example No.4: Different States of Matter

The field of science was developed from the first day humans began asking about phenomena around them. While the results of those inquiries led to social changes, they also promoted the development of science education as a school discipline (Rudolph, 2008). The importance of science education is emphasised even more when we understand that the reciprocal relations between science, social changes and science education also influence the development of other fields such as culture, history, sociology, philosophy and anthropology. Nevertheless, although the core of science education evolves from the desire to better understand the world around us, following students' achievements presents a different picture. Gningue et al. (2013) claimed that throughout their schooling, students are taught the core concepts to investigate their environment, but when they need to ask questions or use the concepts in situations other than science classes, they do not transfer any of their knowledge into practice on a daily basis. Moreover, teachers do not make the links between science and the domains that are influenced by science, a process that might contribute greatly to students' motivation to study and use science in life.

### Data Collection

*Who are the mediatees?* 4th- grade students.

    *Who are the mediators?* The science teacher.

    *What is the content of the mediated interaction?* Science lessons through which the different state of matter are introduced.

### Setting Goals for the Mediated Interaction

Feuerstein's Criteria of *Mediation.*

*Intentionality and reciprocity*: Understanding that the same matter may be found in our environment in different states allow us a better understanding of nature, science and a variety of phenomena around us.

    *Mediation for transcendence*: (1) Cooking an egg is a change of the state of the egg but not of its core ingredients.

(2) When people change their moods they do not change their personality.

*Mediation of meaning*: The environment around me is dynamic and I can adjust to those changes because I can change as well.

*Mediation of awareness of the person as a changing entity*: Changing is a natural process everyone undergoes and it can take place in diverse ways. For example, when I change my opinions in regard to what I want to eat or which movie I wish to see, it doesn't mean I am changed.

Feuerstein's Cognitive Functions.

*Input*: Clear perception of the states we observe, systematic exploration, precise and accurate labelling, well-developed orientation in space and time and the capacity to consider more than one source of information.

*Elaboration*: Accurate definition of the problem that the matter can appear in different forms, selection of relevant cues, using logical evidence to arrive at and defend a conclusion and inferential hypothetical thinking.

*Output*: Using clear and precise language, projection of virtual relationships and precision and accuracy.

Bloom's Taxonomy.

*Knowledge*: Do I recognise different states of matter?

*Comprehension*: Understanding that although there are different states of matter, the core of the matter is the same.

*Application*: Precise labelling of processes and states of matter.

*Analysis*: Investigating each state while focussing on its core and relevant characteristics.

*Synthesis*: Integrating different states to realise what the common matter is.

*Evaluation*: Looking for logical evidences to support the synthesis I conducted before.

Scheme of Planning Mediated Interaction
*Outline of the mediated interaction that includes all the planning parameters, along with examples of bridging transcendence*

Children experience the different states of matters through a range of activities from birth onward. Nevertheless, developing their awareness that certain phenomena around them are different states of matter of the same material has never been done before school science studies. For example, the differences between humidity, rain and hail, or when making jelly, it starts as a liquid but after few minutes develops a firm structure.

Based on the understanding that mediatees come to school after experiencing several natural phenomena in their environment, *mediation* should lead towards developing the logical explanation of these phenomena alongside developing better awareness and understanding of the environment. Hence, I suggest that mediators should begin all science lessons from the mediatees' perspectives, experiences and questions. By doing so, all science lessons will be meaningful for the mediatees and *mediation* for thinking development will be much more efficient.

Following is a mediated interaction I recommend to introduce the content of different states of matter: mediators will ask mediatees to collect information from their parents and siblings in regard to how they used to eat, talk and play when they were 4, 6 and 8 years old. Mediatees will have to organise the information in any way they choose, as long as they present the changes they have undergone in those areas. Then, mediators may ask each of the mediatees an open question such as: how can it be that you are the same person but you act differently? This discussion should lead towards the conclusion, which is the main principle to be used for transcendence in other situations in life, that the same basic material may present different states in different situations.

Reflective Assessment

As mentioned earlier, mediators need to assess their mediated interaction in order to learn from it for their next *mediation* interaction. The main questions that they should ask are: *What did I learn about the mediatees? What did I learn about myself as a mediator? What would I change next time? What would I keep next time?* Answering these questions can be also done by asking the mediatees directly, and then comparing their answers with the reflective perspective of the mediator.

# BIBLIOGRAPHY

Alony, S., & Kozulin, A. (2015). No natural limits: Enhancing language development in children with Down syndrome. *Professional Development Today*, 18(1), 100–106.

Barkley, R. A. (2012). *Executive functions. What they are, how they work, and why they evolved.*New York, NY: Guilford Press.

Batdi, V. (2017). The effect of multiple intelligences on academic achievement: A meta-analytic thematic study. *Educational Sciences: Theory & Practice*, 17(6), 2057–2092.

Bender, W. N., & Crane, D. (2011). *RTI in Math. Practical guidelines for elementary teachers*. Bloomington, IN: Solution Tree Press.

Berninger, V. W., & Abbott, R. D. (1992). The unit of analysis and the constructive processes of the learner: Key concepts for educational neuropsychology. *Educational Psychologists*, 27(2), 223–242.

Biria, R., & Liaghat, F. (2018). Neutralization trade-off effect between accuracy and fluency in EFL writing by mentor text modeling: Cognitive complexity in focus. *International Journal of Applied Linguistics & English Literature*, 7(2), 134–149.

Bloom, B. S. (1956). *Taxonomy of educational objectives, handbook I: The cognitive domain.*New York, NY: Longman.

Borg, S. (2001). Self-perception and practice in teaching grammar. *ELT Journal, 51*(1), 21–29.

Brod, G., Lindenberger, U., Wanger, A. D., & Shing, Y. L. (2016). Knowledge acquisition during exam preparation improves memory and modulates memory formation. *The Journal of Neuroscience, 36*(31), 8103–8111.

Burden, R. (2000). Feuerstein's unique contribution to educational and school psychology. In A. Kozulin & Y. Rand (Eds.), *Experience of mediated learning. An impact of Feuerstein's theory in education and psychology* (pp. 45–54). Kidlington: Elsevier Science.

Cohen, R. A., Mather, N., Schneider, D. A., & White, J. M. (2017). A comparison of school: Teacher knowledge of explicit code-based reading instruction. *Reading and Writing; Dordrecht, 30*(4), 653–690.

Cook, D. A., & Artino, A. R. (2016). Motivation to learn: An overview of contemporary theories. *Medical Education, 50*, 997–1014.

Costa, A. (2000). Mediative environments: Creating conditions for intellectual growth. In A. Kozulin & Y. Rand (Eds.), *Experience of mediated learning. An impact of Feuerstein's theory in education and psychology* (pp. 34–44). Kidlington: Elsevier Science.

Daniels, H. (2016). *Vygotsky and pedagogy.* London: Routledge Publication.

Davis, W. E., Kelley, N. J., Kim, J., Tang, D., & Hicks, J. A. (2016). Motivating the academic mind: High-level construal of academic goals enhances goal meaningfulness, motivation, and self-regulation. *Motivation and Emotion*, *40*, 193–202. doi:10.1007/s11031-015-9522-x

Dewey, J. (1897). My pedagogy creed. *School Journal*, *54*, 77–80.

Dewey, J. (2015). *Experience and education*. New York, NY: Hall-Quest, Free Press (Original work published in 1938).

Draper, A. G., & Moeller, G. H. (1971). We think with words. (Therefore, to improve thinking, teach vocabulary). *The Phi Delta Kappan*, *52*(8), 482–484

Feiler, J. B., & Stabio, M. E. (2018). Three pillars of educational neuroscience form three decades of literature. *Trends in Neuroscience and Education*, *13*, 17–25

Feuerstein, R. (2001). *Mediated learning experience in teaching and counseling*. Jerusalem, Israel: ICELP Publications.

Feuerstein, R., Falik, L., & Feurestein, R. S. (2015). *Changing minds and brains. Higher thinking and cognition through mediated learning*. New York, NY: Teachers College Press.

Feuerstein, R., Feuerstein, R. S., Falik, L., & Rand, Y. (2002). *The dynamic assessment of cognitive modifiability*. Jerusalem, Israel: ICELP Publications.

Feuerstein, R., Feuerstein, R. S., Falik, L., & Rand, Y. (2006). *Creating enhancing cognitive modifiability: The Feuerstein Instrumental Enrichment program*. Jerusalem, Israel: ICELP Publications.

Feuerstein, R., Mintzker, Y., & Feuerstein, R. S. (2001). *Mediated learning experience: Guidelines for parents*. Jerusalem, Israel: ICELP Publications.

Feuerstein, S. (2002). *Biblical and Talmudic antecedents of mediated learning experience theory.* Jerusalem, Israel: ICELP Publications.

Fischer, P. D. (1998). Commercials in the classroom?! What next, *music videos? 'Yes.' Radical Teacher, 52*(April 30), 21–29.

Flavian, H. (2017). Talent development via cognitive mediation. In F. Nafukho, K. Dirani, & B. Irby (Eds.), *Talent development and the global economy* (pp. 155–177). Charlotte, NC: Information Age Publishing.

Flavian, H., & Dan, D. (2018). Assessing teachers' use of language and their teaching quality. *Journal of Quality Assurance in Education, 26*(4), 466–475.

Freeman, R., & Karlsson, F. M. (2012). Strategies for learning experiences in family child care. *Childhood Education, 88*(2), 81–90.

Friedman, I., Grobgeld, E., & Teichman-Weinberg, A. (2019). Imbuing education with brain research can improve teaching and enhance productive learning. *Scientific Research Publishing, Psychology, 10*, 122–131.

Gardner, H. (2000). *The disciplined mind. Beyond facts and standardized tests, the K-12 education that every child deserves.* New York, NY: Penguin Group.

Gardner, H. (2011). *Frames of mind. The theory of multiple intelligences.* New York, NY: Basic Books.

Gningue, S. M., Peach, R., & Schroder, B. (2013). Developing effective mathematics teaching: Assessing content and pedagogical knowledge, student-centered teaching, and student engagement. *The Mathematics Enthusiast; Charlotte: 10*(3), 621–645.

Hadwin, A. F. (2008). Self-regulated learning. In T. L. Good (Ed.), *21ˢᵗ century education: A reference handbook* (pp. 178–183). Thousand Oaks, CA: Sage Publications.

Harris, P. (1997). Piaget in Paris: From "autism" to logic. *Human Development*, *40*(2), 109–123.

Haywood, C. H. (2004). Thinking in, around, and about the curriculum: The role of cognitive education. *International Journal of Disability, Development and Education*, *51*(3), 231–252.

Hickling-Hudson, A., & Hepple, E. (2015). "Come in and look around". Professional development of student teachers through public pedagogy in a library exhibition. *Australian Journal of Adult Learning*, *55*(3), 443–459.

Jackson, P. W. (1990). *John Dewey: The school and society: The child and the curriculum*. Chicago, IL: The University of Chicago Press.

Kozulin, A. (1998). *Psychological tools. A sociocultural approach to education*. London: Harvard University Press.

Kozulin, A. (1999). *Vygotsky's psychology. A biography of ideas*. New York, NY: Harvard University Press.

Kozulin, A. (2000). The diversity of instrumental enrichment applications. In A. Kozulin & Y. Rand (Eds.), *Experience of mediated learning. An impact of Feuerstein's theory in education and psychology* (pp. 257–273). Kidlington: Elsevier Science.

Kozulin, A., & Rand, Y. (2000). *Experience of mediated learning. An impact of Feuerstein's theory in education and psychology*. Kidlington: Elsevier Science.

Langeberg, M. E. (2019). Changing EPP curriculum. An ethnographic study of preservice English teachers and writing feedback methodology. *Issues in Teacher Education*, *28*(1), 36–51.

Lizarrga, M. L. S., Baquedano, M. T. S., & Oliver, M. S. (2010). Psychological intervention in thinking skills with primary education students. *School Psychology International*, *31*, 131–145. doi:10.1177/0143034309352419

Maslow, A. H. (2014). *Toward a psychology of being*. Floyd, VA: Sublime Books.

Mix, K. S., & Cheng, Y. L. (2012). The relation between space and math: Developmental and educational implications. *Advances in Child Development and Behaviour*, *42*, 197–243.

Moyes, R. A. (2014). *Executive function "dysfunction": Strategies for educators and parents*. London: Jessica Kingsley Publishers.

Nigles, L., & Usnick, V. (2000). The role of spatial ability in physical education and mathematics. *Journal of Physical Education, Recreation & Dance*, *71*(6), 29–33.

Piaget, J. (2000). In H. Weaver (Trans.), *The psychology of the child*. New York, NY: Basic Books (Original work published in 1966).

Piaget, J. (2001). In Kegan Paul and Routledge (Trans.), *The psychology of intelligence*. New York, NY: Routledge Classics (Original work published in 1947).

Pink, D. H. (2009). *Drive: The surprising truth about what motivates us*. New York, NY: Riverhead Books.

Reichenberg, R., & Rand, Y. (2000). Reflective teaching and its relation to modes of existence in practical teaching experience. In A. Kozulin & Y. Rand (Eds.), *Experience of mediated learning. An impact of Feuerstein's theory in education and psychology* (pp. 114–133). Kidlington: Elsevier Science.

Rosenberg-Lee, M. (2018). Training studies: An experimental design to advance educational neuroscience. *International Mind, Brain, and Education, 12*(1) 12–22.

Rudolph, J. (2008). Historical writing on science education: A review of the landscape. *Studies in Science Education, 44*(1), 63–82.

Scully, D. (2017). Constructing multiple-choice items to measure higher-order thinking. *Practical Assessment, Research & Evaluation, 22*(4), 1–13.

Sellars, J. (2014). Plato's apology of Socrates: A metaphilosophical text. *Philosophy and Literature, 38*(2), 433–445.

Shayer, M., & Adhami, M. (2010). Realizing the cognitive potential of children 5–7 with a mathematics focus: Post-test long-term effects of a 2-year intervention. *British Journal of Educational Psychology, 80*, 363–379.

Sink, C. A., Edwards, C. N., & Weir, S. J. (2007). Helping children transition from kindergarten to first grade. *Professional School Counseling, 10*(3), 233–237.

Van Der Aalsvoort, G. M., Resing, W. C. M., & Ruijssemaars, A. J. J. M. (Eds.). (2002). *Learning potential assessments and cognitive training: Actual research and perspectives in theory building and methodology.* Kidlington: Elsevier Science.

Weinbaum, D., & Veita, V. (2017). Open ended intelligence: The individuation of intelligent agents. *Journal of Experimental & Theoretical Artificial Intelligence, 29*(2), 371–396.

White, G. (2006). Visual basic programming impact on cognitive development of college students. *Journal of Information Systems Education*, *17*(4), 421–427.

Willis, P. (2007). Transformative pedagogy for social capital. *Australian Journal of Adult Learning*, *47*(3), 349–378.

Zull, J. E. (2011). *From brain to mind. Using neuroscience to guide change in education*. Sterling, VA: Publishing, LLC.

# INDEX

# ABOUT THE AUTHOR

**Dr. Heidi Flavian** is a Senior Lecturer, a Researcher and the Head of Special Education department at Achva Academic College in Israel, and serves as a Senior Lecturer in the International Team in the Feuerstein Institute since 2002. She is also a Co-Editor of the Journal of Quality Assurance in Education, and served as a Guest Editor for the Journal of Quality Assurance in Education in 2018. Her main areas of research and publishing are teacher training, mediation, thinking processes among students, and teaching students with special needs.